Microsoft® Office Word 2007

Level 1 (Second Edition)

Microsoft® Office Word 2007: Level 1 (Second Edition)

Part Number: 084893
Course Edition: 1.2

NOTICES

What is the Microsoft Business Certification Program?

The Microsoft Business Certification Program enables candidates to show that they have something exceptional to offer – proven expertise in Microsoft Office programs. The two certification tracks allow candidates to choose how they want to exhibit their skills, either through validating skills within a specific Microsoft product or taking their knowledge to the next level and combining Microsoft programs to show that they can apply multiple skill sets to complete more complex office tasks. Recognized by businesses and schools around the world, over 3 million certifications have been obtained in over 100 different countries. The Microsoft Business Certification Program is the only Microsoft-approved certification program of its kind.

What is the Microsoft Certified Application Specialist Certification?

Your comments are important to us. Please contact us at Element K Press LLC, 1-800-478-7788, 500 Canal View Boulevard, Rochester, NY 14623, Attention: Product Planning, or through our Web site at **http://support.elementkcourseware.com**.

The Microsoft Certified Application Specialist Certification exams focus on validating specific skill sets within each of the Microsoft® Office system programs. The candidate can choose which exam(s) they want to take according to which skills they want to validate. The available Application Specialist exams include:

- Using Microsoft® Windows Vista™
- Using Microsoft® Office Word 2007
- Using Microsoft® Office Excel® 2007
- Using Microsoft® Office PowerPoint® 2007
- Using Microsoft® Office Access 2007
- Using Microsoft® Office Outlook® 2007

What is the Microsoft Certified Application Professional Certification?

The Microsoft Certified Application Professional Certification exams focus on a candidate's ability to use the 2007 Microsoft® Office system to accomplish industry-agnostic functions, for example Budget Analysis and Forecasting, or Content Management and Collaboration. The available Application Professional exams currently include:

- Organizational Support
- Creating and Managing Presentations
- Content Management and Collaboration
- Budget Analysis and Forecasting

What do the Microsoft Business Certification Vendor of Approved Courseware logos represent?

The logos validate that the courseware has been approved by the Microsoft® Business Certification Vendor program and that these courses cover objectives that will be included in the relevant exam. It also means that after utilizing this courseware, you may be prepared to pass the exams required to become a Microsoft Certified Application Specialist or Microsoft Certified Application Professional.

For more information:

To learn more about Microsoft Certified Application Specialist or Professional exams, visit **www.microsoft.com/learning/msbc**.

To learn about other Microsoft Certified Application Specialist approved courseware from Element K, visit **www.elementkcourseware.com**.

∗ The availability of Microsoft Certified Application exams varies by Microsoft Office program, program version and language. Visit **www.microsoft.com/learning** for exam availability.

Microsoft, the Office Logo, Outlook, and PowerPoint are either registered trademarks or trademarks of Microsoft Corporation in the United States and/or other countries. The Microsoft Certified Application Specialist and Microsoft Certified Application Professional Logos are used under license from Microsoft Corporation.

Microsoft® Office Word 2007: Level 1 (Second Edition)

Microsoft® Office Word 2007: Level 1 (Second Edition)

About This Course

Word processing is the use of computers to create, revise, and save documents for printing and future retrieval. This course is the first in a series of three Microsoft® Office Word 2007 courses. It will provide you with the basic concepts required to produce basic business documents.

This course can benefit you by providing you with basic competence in creating electronic documents for personal and business use by using Microsoft® Word 2007. Historically, documents were painstakingly created and edited by hand. Over time, producing documents has become more efficient. Microsoft® Word 2007 makes creating and editing documents even easier by providing a user-friendly environment, enabling you to add text, graphics, tables, formatting, and more with just a few mouse clicks.

This course can also benefit you if you are preparing to take the Microsoft Certified Application Specialist exam for Microsoft® Word 2007. Please refer to the CD-ROM that came with this course for a document that maps exam objectives to the content in the Microsoft Office Word Courseware series. To access the mapping document, insert the CD-ROM into your CD-ROM drive and at the root of the CD, double-click Exam-Mapping.doc to open the mapping document. In addition to the mapping document, two assessment files per course can be found on the CD-ROM to check your knowledge. To access the assessments, at the root of the course part number folder, double-click 084893s3.doc to view the assessments without the answers marked, or double-click 084893ie.doc to view the assessments with the answers marked.

If your book did not come with a CD, please go to **http:// www.elementk.com/ courseware-file-downloads** to download the data files.

Course Description

Target Student

This course is intended for individuals who want to gain basic knowledge of working on Word. Individuals who want to pursue Microsoft Certified Application Specialist certification in Microsoft Office Word 2007 can also take this course.

Course Prerequisites

Students should be familiar with using personal computers and have used a mouse and keyboard. You should be comfortable in the Windows environment and be able to use Windows to manage information on your computer. Specifically, you should be able to launch and close programs; navigate to information stored on the computer; and manage files and folders. Students should have completed the following courses or possess equivalent knowledge before starting with this course:

■ *Windows XP Professional: Level 1*

■ *Windows XP Professional: Level 2*

■ *Windows XP: Introduction*

■ *Windows 2000: Introduction*

How to Use This Book

As a Learning Guide

Each lesson covers one broad topic or set of related topics. Lessons are arranged in order of increasing proficiency with *Microsoft® Word 2007*; skills you acquire in one lesson are used and developed in subsequent lessons. For this reason, you should work through the lessons in sequence.

We organized each lesson into results-oriented topics. Topics include all the relevant and supporting information you need to master *Microsoft® Word 2007*, and activities allow you to apply this information to practical hands-on examples.

Have the opportunity to try out each new skill on a specially prepared sample file. This saves you typing time and allows you to concentrate on the skill at hand. Through the use of sample files, hands-on activities, illustrations that give you feedback at crucial steps, and supporting background information, this book provides you with the foundation and structure to learn *Microsoft® Word 2007* quickly and easily.

As a Review Tool

Any method of instruction is only as effective as the time and effort you are willing to invest in it. In addition, some of the information that you learn in class may not be important to you immediately, but it may become important later on. For this reason, we encourage you to spend some time reviewing the topics and activities after the course. For additional challenge when reviewing activities, try the "What You Do" column before looking at the "How You Do It" column.

As a Reference

The organization and layout of the book make it easy to use as a learning tool and as an after-class reference. You can use this book as a first source for definitions of terms, background information on given topics, and summaries of procedures.

Course Icons

Icon	Description
	A **Caution Note** makes students aware of potential negative consequences of an action, setting, or decision that are not easily known.
	Display Slide provides a prompt to the instructor to display a specific slide. Display Slides are included in the Instructor Guide only.
	An **Instructor Note** is a comment to the instructor regarding delivery, classroom strategy, classroom tools, exceptions, and other special considerations. Instructor Notes are included in the Instructor Guide only.
	Notes Page indicates a page that has been left intentionally blank for students to write on.
	A **Student Note** provides additional information, guidance, or hints about a topic or task.
	A **Version Note** indicates information necessary for a specific version of software.

Certification

This course is designed to help you prepare for the following certification.

Certification Path: Microsoft Certified Application Specialist – Word 2007

This course is one of a series of Element K courseware titles that addresses Microsoft Certified Application Specialist (Microsoft Business Certification) skill sets. The Microsoft Certified Application Specialist program is for individuals who use Microsoft's business desktop software and who seek recognition for their expertise with specific Microsoft products. Certification candidates must pass one or more proficiency exams in order to earn Microsoft Certified Application Specialist certification.

Course Objectives

In this course, you will create, edit, and enhance standard business documents using Microsoft® Office Word 2007.

You will:

- create a basic document using Microsoft Word.
- edit documents by locating and modifying text.
- format text.
- format paragraphs.
- add tables to a document.
- add graphic elements to a document.
- control a document's page setup and its overall appearance.
- proof documents to make them more accurate.

Course Requirements

Hardware

For this course, you will need one computer for each student and one for the instructor. Each computer will need the following minimum hardware components:

- A 1 GHz Pentium-class processor or faster.
- A minimum of 256 MB of RAM. 512 MB of RAM is recommended.
- A 10 GB hard disk or larger. You should have at least 1 GB of free hard disk space available for the Office installation.
- A CD-ROM drive.
- A keyboard and mouse or other pointing device.
- A 1024 x 768 resolution monitor is recommended.
- Network cards and cabling for local network access.
- Internet access (contact your local network administrator).
- A printer (optional) or an installed printer driver.
- A projection system to display the instructor's computer screen.

Software

- Microsoft® Office Professional Plus 2007 Edition.
- Microsoft Office Suite Service Pack 1
- Windows XP Professional with Service Pack 2.

  This course was developed using the Windows XP operating system; however, the manufacturer's documentation states that it will also run on Vista. If you use Vista, you might notice some slight differences when keying the course.

Class Setup

For Initial Class Setup

1. Install Windows XP Professional on an empty partition.

    - Leave the Administrator password blank.

    - For all other installation parameters, use values that are appropriate for your environment (see your local network administrator for details).

2. On Windows XP Professional, disable the Welcome screen. (This step ensures that students will be able to log on as the Administrator user regardless of what other user accounts exist on the computer.)

    a. Click Start and choose Control Panel→User Accounts.

    b. Click Change The Way Users Log On And Off.

    c. Uncheck Use Welcome Screen.

    d. Click Apply Options.

3. On Windows XP Professional, install Service Pack 2. Use the Service Pack installation defaults.

4. On the computer, install a printer driver (a physical print device is optional). Click Start and choose Printers And Faxes. Under Printer Tasks, click Add A Printer and follow the prompts.

    If you do not have a physical printer installed, right-click the printer and choose Pause Printing to prevent any print error messages.

5. Run the Internet Connection Wizard to set up the Internet connection as appropriate for your environment, if you did not do so during installation.

6. Display known file type extensions.

    a. Open Windows Explorer (right-click Start and then select Explore).

    b. Choose Tools→Folder Options.

    c. On the View tab, in the Advanced Settings list box, uncheck Hide Extensions For Known File Types.

    d. Click Apply, and then click OK.

    e. Close Windows Explorer.

7. Log on to the computer as the Administrator user if you have not already done so.

8. Perform a Complete installation of Microsoft Office Professional 2007.

9. Install Microsoft Office Suite Service Pack 1.

10. In the User Name dialog box, click OK to accept the default user name and initials.

11. In the Microsoft Office 2007 Activation Wizard dialog box, click Next to activate the Office 2007 application.

12. When the activation of Microsoft Office 2007 is complete, click Close to close the Microsoft Office 2007 Activation Wizard dialog box.

13. In the User Name dialog box, click OK.

14. In the Welcome To Microsoft 2007! dialog box, click Finish. You must have an active Internet connection in order to complete this step. Here, you select the Download And Install Updates From Microsoft Update When Available (Recommended) option, so that whenever there is a new update, it gets automatically installed in your system.

15. After the Microsoft Update runs, in the Microsoft Office dialog box, click OK.

16. Minimize the Language Bar, if necessary.

17. On the course CD-ROM, open the 084_893 folder. Then, open the Data folder. Run the 084893dd.exe self-extracting file located within. This will install a folder named 084893Data on your C drive. This folder contains all the data files that you will use to complete this course.

Within each lesson folder, you may find a Solution folder. This folder contains solution files for the lesson's activities and lesson lab, which can be used by students to check their end results.

If your book did not come with a CD, please go to **http:// www.elementk.com/ courseware-file-downloads** to download the data files.

Customize the Windows Desktop

Customize the Windows desktop to display the My Computer and My Network Places icon on the student and instructor systems:

1. Right-click the Desktop and choose Properties.

2. Select the Desktop tab.

3. Click Customize Desktop.

4. In the Desktop Items dialog box, check My Computer and My Network Places.

5. Click OK and click Apply.

6. Close the Display Properties dialog box.

Before Every Class

1. Log on to each computer as the Administrator user.

2. Delete the existing C:\084893Data folder and extract a fresh copy of the course data files from the CD-ROM provided with the course.

3. In Microsoft Word, reset the Results Should Be options in the Clip Art task pane to All Media Types.

    a. In the Clip Art task pane, display the Results Should Be drop-down list.

    b. Select All Media Types.

    c. To clear "money" from the search list, search for "house".

    d. Close the Clip Art task pane.

4. Open the AutoCorrect Options dialog box, and select and delete the bp/Burke Properties entry and the frf/Facilities Request Form entry.

5. Open the Research Options dialog box, click Update/Remove, and select and remove the Factiva iWorks service.

6. For the Save category of the Word Options dialog box, set the default file location to C:\Documents and Settings\Administrator\My Documents.

7. For the Customize category of the Word Options dialog box, reset the Quick Access toolbar.

8. For the Proofing category of the Word Options dialog box, uncheck Show Readability Statistics.

9. To eliminate any changes students might have inadvertently made to the Normal template, re-create the Normal.dotm template:

    a. Close Word.

    b. Delete C:\Documents and Settings\Administrator\Application Data\Microsoft\ Templates\Normal.dotm.

    c. Re-open Word.

10. If you have a printer driver installed and paused rather than printing to a physical printer, clear all documents from the print queue:

    a. Open the Printers or Printers And Faxes window.

    b. Right-click the printer.

    c. Choose Cancel All Documents.

    d. Click Yes and close the window.

List of Additional Files

Printed with each activity is a list of files students open to complete that activity. Many activities also require additional files that students do not open, but are needed to support the file(s) students are working with. These supporting files are included with the student data files on the course CD-ROM or data disk. Do not delete these files.

1 Creating a Basic Document

Lesson Time: 1 hour(s), 15 minutes

Lesson Objectives:

In this lesson, you will create a basic document using Microsoft Word.

You will:

- Explore the Microsoft Office Word 2007 user interface, including the Ribbon.
- Open and view a document.
- Customize the Word environment.
- Use Microsoft Office Word Help.
- Enter text.
- Save a document.
- Preview and print a document.

Introduction

Perhaps you have been handwriting letters or using a typewriter to create your personal and business documents. Microsoft® Office Word 2007, with its streamlined user interface and a host of editing and layout tools, makes the authoring experience simpler and more efficient. In this lesson, you will create a document using Word 2007.

No matter what profession you are in, the process of learning something new requires some basic skills to perform even the most common tasks. Learning a new computer program is no different. Time spent familiarizing yourself with Word as you create a basic document will help you acquire the fundamental skills you need to create more complex documents.

TOPIC A

Explore the User Interface

Before you start working in Word, you need to be aware of the various features that are available in the interface. In this topic, you will explore the user interface.

While working on new software, you could potentially waste a significant amount of time searching for specific options in the work environment. You can prevent this by familiarizing yourself with the user interface elements. This will help you achieve the output that you are seeking when you eventually begin using the software.

Microsoft Office Word 2007

Microsoft Office Word 2007 is a program used to create, revise, and save documents for printing, distribution, or future retrieval. Word's tools can help you make your documents more accurate, concise, and correct. The Word interface consists of various elements, such as the Office button, Ribbon, Quick Access toolbar, Microsoft Office Status Bar, as well as others. Microsoft Word is part of the Microsoft Office system, a collection of services and programs that work together to help you perform computing tasks.

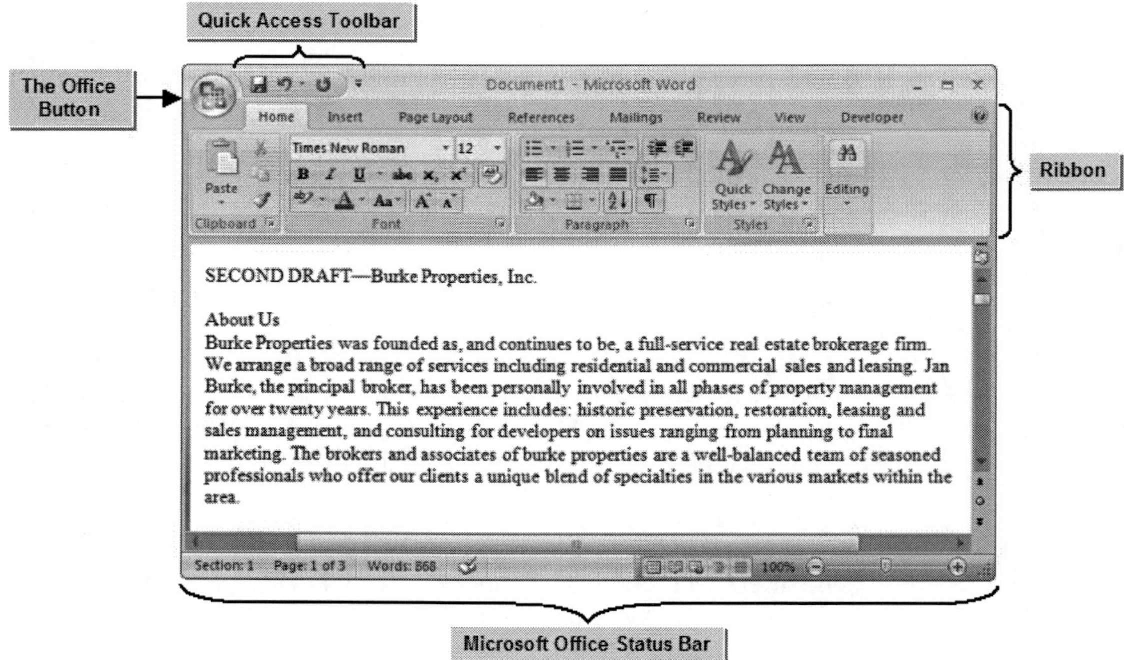

Figure 1-1: Microsoft Office Word interface elements.

Mouse Pointer Shapes

As you use Word, you will notice that the mouse pointer changes shape, depending on where it is located in the program window.

Mouse Pointer Shape	*Description*
I	In the text area, the I-beam mouse pointer is used to indicate the point where text, graphics, tables, and pictures are to be inserted. It is also used to select text.
	Outside the text area, the right-arrow mouse pointer is used to select menu commands, toolbars, buttons, and others.
	On the selection bar, the left-arrow mouse pointer is used to select lines, paragraphs, and the entire document.
	On links, the hand-shaped mouse pointer is used to display more information.

ScreenTips

As you position the mouse pointer over items, such as toolbar buttons, in the program window, Word may display a descriptive label called a *ScreenTip*. You can use a ScreenTip to identify program window items or to help you distinguish between similar looking items. You can customize ScreenTips on the Personalize tab of the Word Options dialog box by selecting any of the following options:

Option	*Description*
Show Feature Description In ScreenTips	Selecting this option displays the name of the element along with a brief description. This option is active by default.
Don't Show Feature Description In ScreenTips	Selecting this option displays the name of the element alone.
Don't Show ScreenTips	Selecting this option disables ScreenTips.

Word Documents

Definition:

A *Word document* is a document that is created using the Microsoft Office Word software. It is a collection of pages containing information in the form of text, pictures, graphics, tables, or charts that is stored in an electronic form in a computer. You can customize document pages according to your needs. The default file format for a Word document created using Microsoft Office Word 2007 is .docx.

Example:

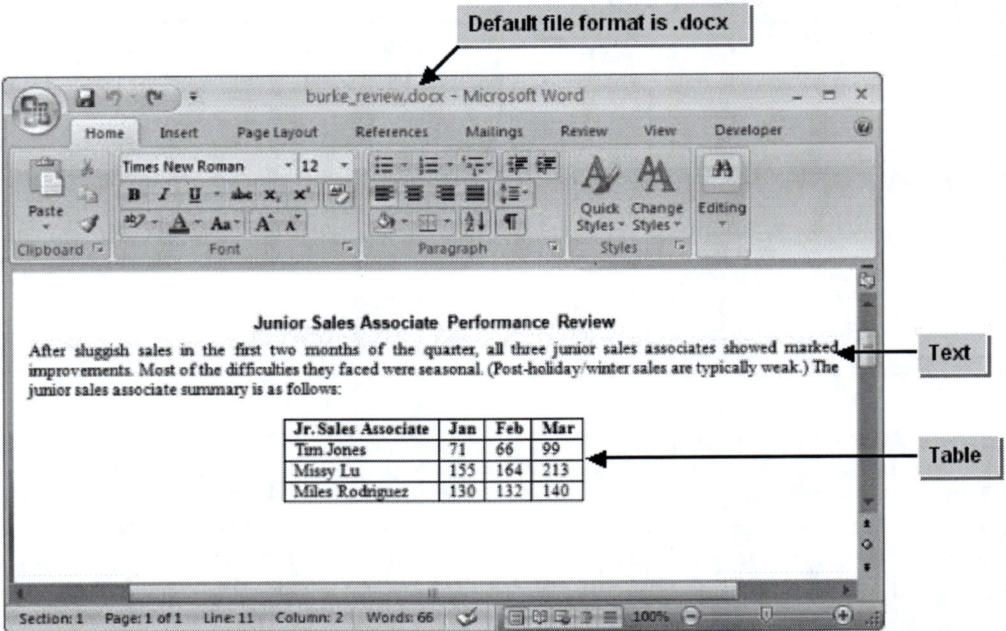

Figure 1-2: A Word document.

The Office Button

Click the *Office button*, located at the top-left corner of the Word interface, to display the Office Menu, a set of options that can be applied to a document as a whole.

Option	Description
New	Opens the New Document dialog box from which you can select either a blank document, a new blog entry, or a blank template.
Open	Opens existing documents, regardless of the version in which they were created.
Save	Saves a document in the .docx format by default.
Save As	Saves a document in formats other than the default file format and also in a different location.
Print	Allows you to preview and print documents.
Prepare	Provides sub-options to check if a document is ready to be shared.
Send	Allows you to send your document either through email or fax.
Publish	Allows you to share your documents with other people through the web.
Close	Closes documents that are open. If the document hasn't been saved, the Microsoft Office Word message box will appear, enabling you to save your document with the latest changes.
Recent Documents	Lists the documents that were recently opened.
Word Options	Opens a dialog box, listing options to customize the Word environment.
Exit Word	Closes the Word application.

The Quick Access Toolbar

By default, the *Quick Access toolbar* is displayed at the top-left corner of the window, above the Ribbon. It provides easy access to core commands such as save a document, undo a previous action, and repeat a previous action. You can customize this toolbar to include other options based on user requirements. The Quick Access toolbar can be placed below the Ribbon.

The Microsoft Office Status Bar

The *Microsoft Office Status Bar* appears at the bottom of the application window, and displays a number of options relating to overall document functionality.

Frame Option	Description
Page Number	Displays the current page number of the document that you are working on.
Live Word Count	Displays the word count in a document as you are typing in it.
Contextual Spell Checker	Checks for proofing errors in a document. A red checked sign denotes the presence of errors that have to be corrected in the document.
Tracked Changes Off/On	Switches on or switches off the track changes mode while you are reviewing or editing a document.
Document Views	Displays a document as it will appear when printed or displayed on a web page. You can also view a document's outline for an overview of the available content.
Zoom Controls	Enables you to zoom in to specific portions of the document that you might want to view and work on. It also enables you to view several pages at the same time to get an overall perspective of the layout.

The Ribbon

The *Ribbon* is a panel at the top portion of a Word document and it contains a selection of easy-to-browse commands that you may need in order to work on a document. It has seven tabs that are organized in the order in which they will be used during document creation. Each of these tabs is divided into groups containing features designed to perform specific tasks during the authoring process. You can hide the Ribbon by double-clicking any active tab.

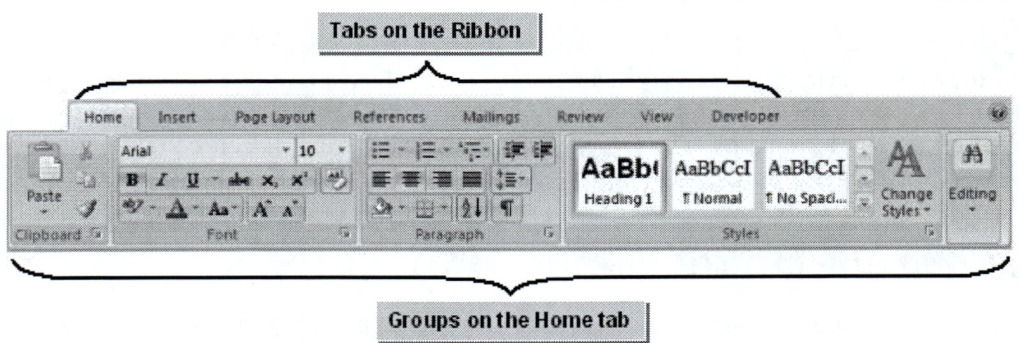

Figure 1-3: The Ribbon in Microsoft Office Word 2007.

Ribbon Buttons

The commands in the different groups of a tab are divided into large and small buttons. While the large buttons determine features that are commonly used, the smaller buttons represent minor features that are designed to work together to achieve a common result.

Tabs on the Ribbon

There are many useful functions on the Home, Insert, Page Layout, Review, and View tabs on the Ribbon.

Tab Name	Description
Home	The *Home tab* contains the most commonly used commands that enable you to start working with a Word document. This tab contains functional groups that allow you to format and edit text. Groups on the Home tab include Clipboard, Font, Paragraph, Styles, and Editing.
Insert	The *Insert tab* contains functional groups that enable quick access to different object types such as charts, tables, and pictures that can be added to a document. Groups on the Insert tab include Pages, Tables, Illustrations, Links, Header and Footer, Text, and Symbols.
Page Layout	The *Page Layout tab* contains functional groups that are used to customize the pages in a document. The placement of text and graphics can also be controlled using the commands on this tab. Groups on the Page Layout tab include Themes, Page Setup, Page Background, Paragraph, and Arrange.
Review	The *Review tab* contains functional groups with various options to review and edit the contents in a document. Groups on the Review tab include Proofing, Comments, Tracking, Changes, Compare, and Protect.
View	The *View tab* contains functional groups with various options that enable you to switch between different document views. Groups on the View tab include Document Views, Show/Hide, Zoom, Window, and Macros.

Task Panes

Definition:

A *task pane* is a small window within the Word environment that provides a list of feature-specific options and commands. Unlike dialog boxes, which provide controls for configuring program or feature settings, task panes generally present a list of choices for inserting or applying items to documents. The task pane is small enough to keep open as you work with your document. You can open task panes from specific groups on the Ribbon and sometimes from within other task panes.

Example:

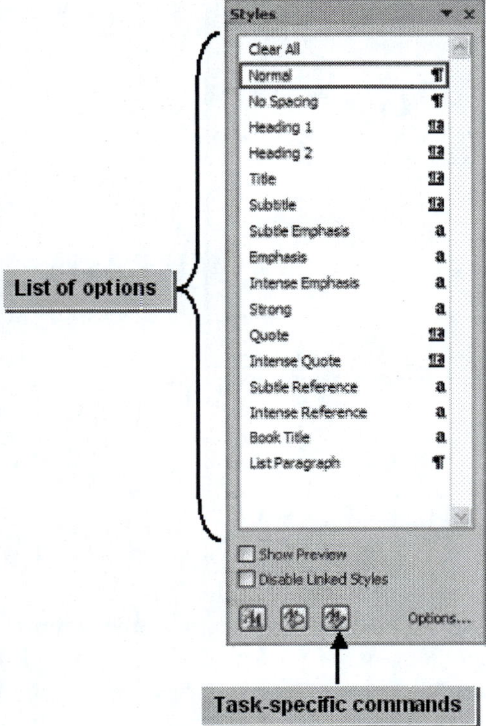

Figure 1-4: A task pane.

Dialog Box Launchers

Definition:

Dialog Box Launchers are small arrow buttons occupying the bottom-right corner of certain groups on the Ribbon. They launch dialog boxes or task panes with commands specific to the features found in that group. These commands are used to adjust the settings that are not available on the Ribbon.

Example:

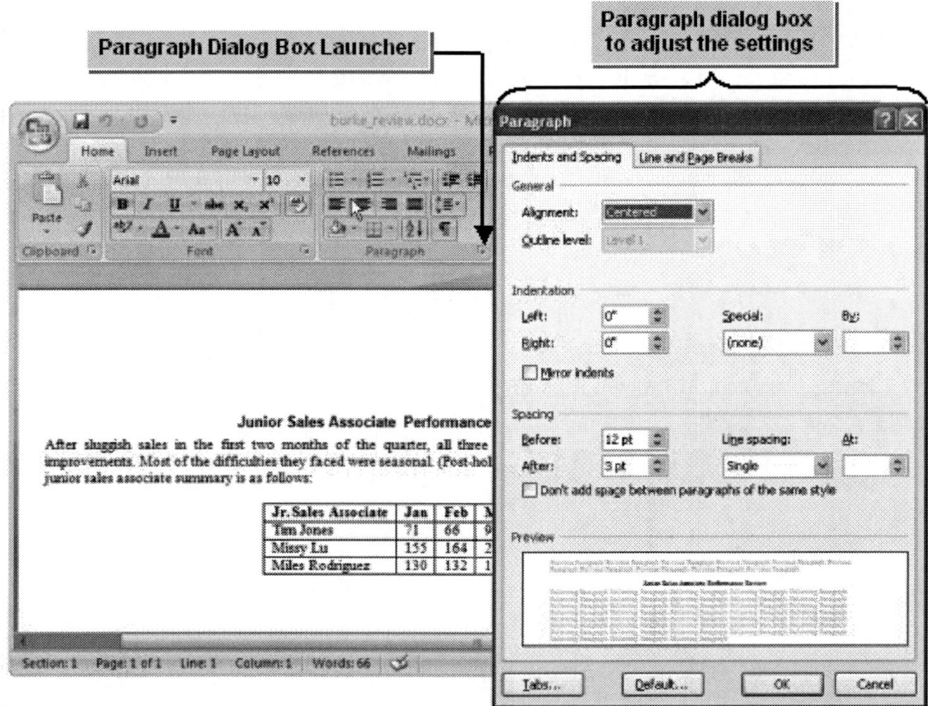

Figure 1-5: *A dialog box launcher.*

Galleries

Definition:

Galleries are libraries that list the varying outcomes of using certain commands found within the Ribbon. They support several layouts by putting together a variety of predefined text styles, table formats, or graphical effects. These effects can also be customized. Galleries are arranged either in a grid or menu-like layout.

Example:

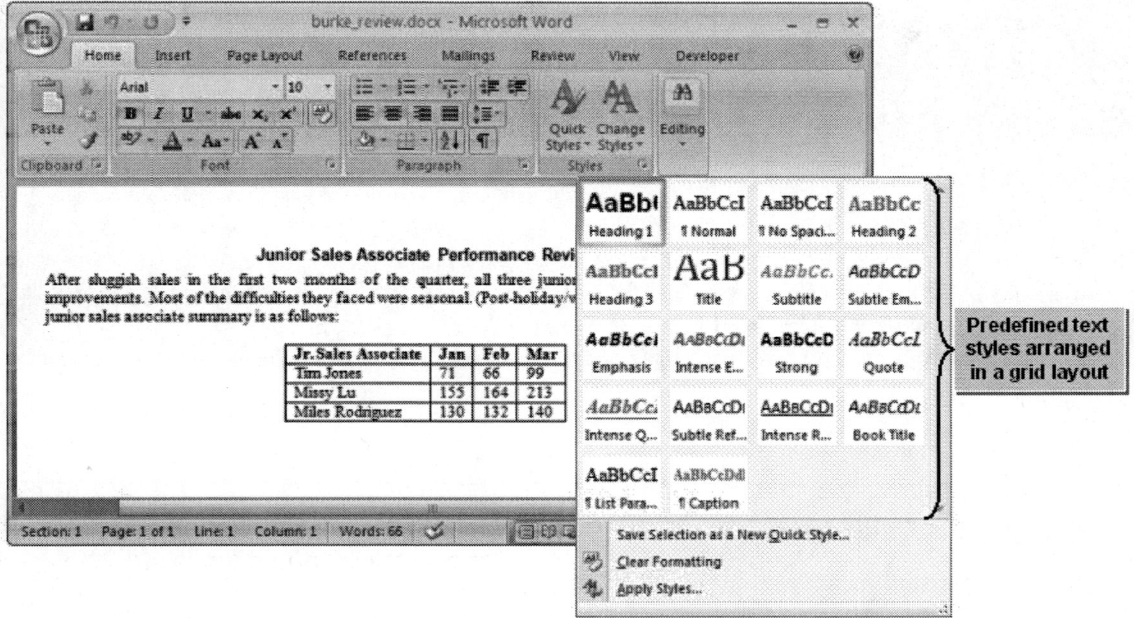

Figure 1-6: The Styles gallery in Word 2007.

Live Preview

Some galleries support *Live Preview*, a feature that enables users to preview the results of applying design and formatting changes to a document, without actually applying it. These changes are displayed in the document as soon as the user moves the mouse pointer over the available options in a gallery.

ACTIVITY 1-1

Exploring Word's User Interface Elements

Scenario:

Your company has just purchased and installed the Microsoft Office Word 2007 application. Henceforth, your manager expects you to use this software to create documents. As you will be working on Word frequently, you decide to spend some time exploring the user interface elements of the Word environment.

What You Do	How You Do It
1. Examine the Office menu.	a. **Choose Start→All Programs→Microsoft Office→Microsoft Office Word 2007.**
	b. In the Microsoft Word window, at the top-left corner, **click the Office button** to display the Office Menu. 
	c. In the document, **click anywhere away from the menu** to close the menu.
2. Examine the groups on the Ribbon.	a. On the Ribbon, the Home tab includes various groups such as Clipboard, Font, Paragraph, and others. **Select the Insert tab** to see the available groups on that tab.
	b. On the Ribbon, **select other tabs** to see the available groups.
3. Examine the Page Setup dialog box.	a. On the Ribbon, **select the Page Layout tab.**
	b. At the bottom-right corner of the Page Setup group, **click the Dialog Box Launcher button.**
	c. **Click Cancel** to close the dialog box.

4. **Display the Page Colors gallery.**

a. In the Page Background group, **click Page Color** to display the Page Colors gallery.

b. In the Standard Colors section, **position the mouse pointer over the fifth color** to view the document in Light Green.

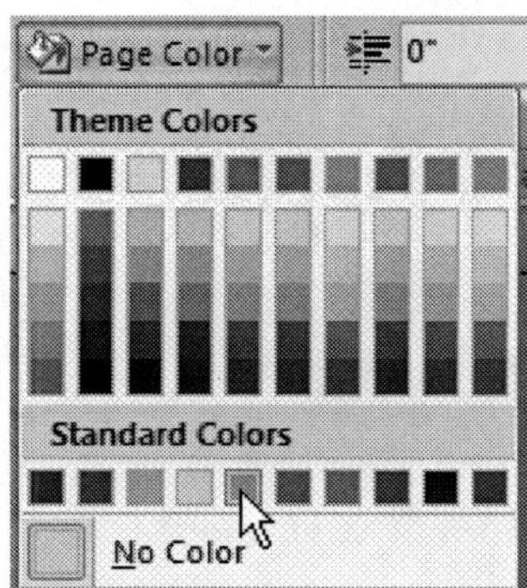

c. To close the gallery, **click anywhere in the document.**

5. **Close the Word document and application.**

a. **Click the Office button and choose Close** to close the document.

b. To close the Word application, **click the Office button and click Exit Word.**

TOPIC B

Open and View a Document

You have explored the user interface. Before you start working on any document, you should be able to identify the appropriate view in which your document should be displayed. In this topic, you will view a document in different view modes.

Your manager has asked you to view the report that he has sent you. Word 2007 provides options to view the document in different view modes and display the document in a mode that best suits your requirements.

Document Views

At the bottom of the Microsoft Office Status Bar there are options that enable users to view a Word document in different view modes.

> The view options at the bottom of the Microsoft Office Status Bar are shortcuts to the commands found on the View tab of the Ribbon.

Document View	*View of the document as it will appear:*
Print Layout	When printed. All sections, such as tables, text, graphics, and images, will appear in their correct positions in the document.
Full Screen Reading	Full length on screen. This view is ideal for viewing two pages at a time.
Web Layout	In a web browser. In this view, the entire document appears on a single page, with tables and text wrapping to fit into the window.
Outline	In outline form, with bullets and plus signs that can be used to hide or display subordinate levels of text.
Draft	In draft view, without pictures and layouts. In this view, the focus is on the text alone.

> In Outline view, the Outlining tab appears as part of the Ribbon. In this tab, you can manipulate the existing outline by changing the heading or body text level of the chosen content and formatting it.

How to Open and View a Document

Procedure Reference: Open a Document and Set the View Mode

To open a document and set the view mode:

1. Open a file you have viewed.

    *   Click the Office button and choose the document from the Recent Documents section.

    *   Or, click the Office button and choose Open.

        a. In the Open dialog box, click the Look In drop-down arrow and navigate to the location of the document you want to open.

        b. Select the desired Word document and click Open.

    *   Or, press Ctrl+O.

        a. In the Open dialog box, click the Look In drop-down arrow and navigate to the location of the document you want to open.

        b. Select the desired Word document and click Open.

2. On the Microsoft Office Status Bar, click a view button to view the document in the desired form.

ACTIVITY 1-2

Viewing a Document

Data Files:

About Us.docx

Scenario:

Your company is hosting a new website and you have been asked to review the write-up on the company. You use Word 2007 to view this document in different view modes to identify the one that best suits your requirements.

What You Do	How You Do It
1. Open an existing document.	a. **Open Microsoft Word.**
	b. **Click the Office button and choose Open.**
	c. In the Open dialog box, **navigate to C:\ 084893Data\Creating a Basic Document.**
	d. **Select About Us.docx.**
	e. **Click Open.**
2. View the document in different view modes.	a. On the Microsoft Office Status Bar, **click the Web Layout button** to change to Web Layout view.
	b. On the Microsoft Office Status Bar, **click the Outline button** to change to Outline view.
	c. On the Microsoft Office Status Bar, **click the Print Layout button** to return to Print Layout view.
	d. On the Microsoft Office Status Bar, **click the Zoom In button** to magnify the document to 110 percent.
	e. **Close the Word document.**

TOPIC C
Customize the Word Environment

You have worked with a few of the Word 2007 user interface elements. If you are not comfortable working with the display and arrangement of the default interface elements in Word, you may wish to personalize them to suit your requirements. In this topic, you will customize the Word environment.

When you start working with new software, the interface may not contain all the options that you require or sometimes it may be cluttered with options that you may not require at all. This will slow you down and make working a cumbersome process. By customizing the environment, you will be able to display only those options that you need for your current workflow.

The Word Options Dialog Box

The *Word Options dialog box* contains a series of tabs, each of which contains commands required to customize the Word environment.

Tab	*Enables You To*
Popular	Personalize your work environment by setting options, such as language, color scheme, user name, and others. It also allows you to enable the Live Preview feature.
Display	Modify how the text content is displayed on screen and in the print version. You can opt to show or hide certain page elements, such as Highlighter Marks and Formatting Marks.
Proofing	Specify how Word should correct and format text that you type. You can set auto correction settings and ensure that Word corrects all spelling and grammatical errors. You can also ensure that Word ignores certain words or errors in a document.
Save	Select customization options to save documents. Depending on how often you want to save backup information for your documents, you can specify how frequently a document will be auto saved. You can also change the locations of where these drafts are saved.
Advanced	Select advanced options needed to work with Word. You can specify options for editing, copying, pasting, displaying, printing, saving, and writing content.
Customize	Customize the Quick Access toolbar. Using this tab, you can select those commands that you want added to the Quick Access toolbar. You can also opt to position the Quick Access toolbar below the Ribbon.
Add-Ins	Manage Office add-ins if you are using extensions to enhance Office applications. Add-ins extend the capabilities of a function. Many of these add-ins are installed with Office 2007.
Trust Center	Keep the system and documents in it safe. Using the Advanced Trust Center Settings button on this tab, you can set the security measures needed to keep a document secure.
Resources	Communicate with Microsoft for support, updates, or on how to rectify problems in Office applications.

How to Customize the Word Environment

Procedure Reference: Customize the Quick Access Toolbar

To customize the Quick Access toolbar:

1. Click the Office button and click Word Options.

2. In the Word Options dialog box, select the Customize category.

3. In the Choose Commands From drop-down list, select the category from which the command is to be added to the Quick Access toolbar.

4. In the list box, select the desired command from the chosen category and click Add.

5. If necessary, check the Show Quick Access Toolbar Below The Ribbon check box to display the Quick Access toolbar below the Ribbon.

6. Click OK to close the Word Options dialog box.

You can also click the Customize Quick Access Toolbar button to customize the Quick Access toolbar.

7. On the Ribbon, select the desired tab, right-click the name of the desired group and choose Add To Quick Access toolbar to add the group to the Quick Access toolbar.

You can add any number of groups to the Quick Access toolbar. However, the Ribbon cannot be added to the Quick Access toolbar.

Customizing the Microsoft Office Status Bar

To show or hide options on the Status Bar, right-click the Status Bar and check or uncheck the desired options.

Minimizing the Ribbon

Although it is not possible to move or hide the Ribbon, you can minimize it so that you will have more space available in your work area. To minimize the Ribbon, you can select Minimize The Ribbon from the Customize Quick Access Toolbar drop-down list. You can also double-click the active tab on the Ribbon or press Ctrl+F1. The interface now only displays the tabs and the corresponding groups and galleries are hidden. To view the Ribbon, click any tab. To restore the Ribbon, double-click any tab.

Procedure Reference: Customize the Save Options

To customize the save options:

1. Open the Word Options dialog box and select the Save category.

2. In the Customize How Documents Are Saved pane, in the Save Documents section, customize the save options. You can choose a default file type and file save location, a location for files that Word automatically recovers after a program crash, and a time interval at which Word should save autorecovery information.

3. Click OK to close the Word Options dialog box.

ACTIVITY 1-3

Customizing the Microsoft Office Word User Interface

Data Files:

Nolan Letter.docx

Scenario:

You have just finished your work on the About Us document and wish to work on the Nolan Letter document. You feel that displaying frequently used commands such as New, Open, and Close on the interface will increase your efficiency in Word. You also wish to add the paragraph group to the interface. Your company insists on maintaining all official files in a specific folder on the C drive. You wish to set this as your default save location.

What You Do	How You Do It
1. **Add the necessary commands to the Quick Access toolbar.**	a. **Click the Office button and choose Word Options.**
	b. In the Word Options dialog box, **select the Customize category.**
	c. In the list box below the Choose Commands From drop-down list, **select Open.**
	d. **Click Add** to add the Open command to the Quick Access toolbar.
	e. In the list box below the Choose Commands From drop-down list, **select New and click Add.**
	f. From the Choose Commands From drop-down list, **select Office Menu.**
	g. In the list box below the Choose Commands From drop-down list, **select Close and click Add.**
	h. **Click OK** to close the Word Options dialog box.

	i.	**Verify that the commands appear on the Quick Access toolbar.**

2.	**Open the Nolan Letter document using the Quick Access toolbar.**	a.	On the Quick Access toolbar, **click the Open button.**
		b.	In the Open dialog box, **navigate to C:\ 084893Data\Creating a Basic Document.**
		c.	**Select Nolan Letter.docx.**
		d.	**Click Open.**

3.	**Add the Paragraph group to the Quick Access toolbar.**	a.	On the Home tab of the Ribbon, in the Paragraph group, **right-click the word Paragraph in the Paragraph group and choose Add To Quick Access Toolbar.**
		b.	On the Quick Access toolbar, **click the Paragraph group button** to open the Paragraph group.
		c.	All the Paragraph group options are now available from the Quick Access toolbar. **Click the Paragraph group button again** to close the Paragraph group.

4.	**Set Word's default save location.**	a.	**Click the Office button and choose Word Options.**
		b.	In the Word Options dialog box, **select the Save category.**
		c.	In the Save Documents section, in the Default File Location text box, select the existing location **and type *C:\084893Data* and click OK.**
		d.	On the Quick Access toolbar, **click the Close button** to close the document.

TOPIC D
Obtain Help

In the previous topic, you configured the Word user interface to make your document-editing tasks more efficient. Another way you can work efficiently is to use the Microsoft Word online Help system to find information or to answer questions that might arise as you work. In this topic, you will use Word's built-in Help system to get assistance when you have a query.

Word's built-in Help system enables you to help yourself whenever you have Word-related questions. As a result, you no longer need to rely on your coworkers or technical support. You can find the answers for all your queries quickly and easily. The Help system can increase your knowledge of Word.

Word Help

The *Word Help* feature is a complete user manual on the functionality of the various features of Microsoft Office Word 2007. The Word Help window provides a quick and easy way to find answers to Word-related queries, online or offline. You can also search for information by browsing through the links that are already provided or by typing in a keyword.

Wildcard Characters

A Wildcard is a special symbol that stands for one or more characters. For example, the symbol asterisk (*) is a wildcard that stands for any combination of letters. Word Help does not qualify wildcard characters as searchable text.

Word Help Options

In the Word Help window, there are a number of options that allow you to find answers for all your Word-related queries.

Option	Description
Word Help toolbar	Provides access to navigational, print, and format commands.
Type Words To Search For text box	Allows you to type the keyword on which you need to search for information. Previously asked questions can be found in the Search Criteria drop-down list.
Search drop-down list	Provides you options, based on the criterion you have chosen, to search for Help information from online or offline content.
Table Of Contents pane	Lists the topics available in Word Help as various categories. You can choose to either show or hide the Table Of Contents pane.
Browse Word Help pane	Displays the topics available on Word Help in a tabular form. You can navigate to a topic by clicking it.

Word Help Toolbar Options

On the Word Help toolbar, there are buttons that enable you to navigate through Help. For example, you can move back and forth between pages, stop a search in progress, display the Help Home page or Table of Contents, or print a particular Help topic. You can also control the Help display by increasing or decreasing the size of the text or by setting the Help window to stay on top of other windows.

Word Help with Areas of Search

In Word Help, you can specify the area of search to narrow down the search results to a specific area. Areas of search can be either offline or online.

The following table gives a brief description of the areas of search in Word.

Area Of Search	Option Lists
All Word	Information on the keyword from the built-in Help and takes you to the Office online website, if required.
Word Help	Information on the keyword from the built-in Help as well as the Office online website, but does not take you to the Office online website.
Word Templates	Sample templates that are available on the Office online website.
Word Training	Sample training information from the Office online website.
Developer Reference	Programming tasks, samples, and references to create customized solutions.

How to Use Microsoft Office Word Help

Procedure Reference: Find Information in Word Help

To find information in Word Help:

1. To open the Word Help window, click the Help button on the Ribbon, or press F1.
2. If desired, click the Show Table Of Contents button to display the Table of Contents.
3. Click a link to view its details.
   - In the Table Of Contents pane, click a link to view its details.
   - Or, click a link in the Browse Word Help pane to view its details.
4. If desired, search for information.
   a. To narrow the search to a particular area, select an option from the Search drop-down list.
   b. In the Type Words To Search For text box, type a keyword.
   c. Click Search to display the search results.

Keeping the Microsoft Office Help Window on Top

You can set the Microsoft Office Help window so that it stays on top of the Word window or other Microsoft Office windows. To determine the current mode, point to the Not On Top/Keep On Top button. The ScreenTip should tell you the mode the Help window is in. To toggle to the other mode, click the button.

ACTIVITY 1-4

Finding Information in Word Help

Scenario:
There are new editorial guidelines that will require you to add page numbers to most documents. As a relatively new user of Word, you do not know how to go about inserting page numbers in a Word document.

What You Do	**How You Do It**
1. **Display the Word Help window.**	a. At the top-right corner of the Ribbon, **click the Microsoft Office Word Help button.**
	b. At the top-right corner of the Word Help window, **click the Maximize button.**
	c. On the toolbar, **click the Show Table Of Contents button** to display the Table of Contents.
2. **Browse and search for Help information.**	a. In the Word Help window, in the Browse Word Help section, **click the Viewing And Navigating link.**
	b. The topics on viewing and navigating appear. In the Type Words To Search For text box, **click and type *insert page numbers***
	insert page numbers
	c. **Click the Search drop-down arrow.**
	d. In the Content From This Computer section, **select Word Help.**
	e. **Click Search** to display links related to Insert Page Numbers.
	f. **Click the Insert Page Numbers Help link** to view the Help information.

<table>
<tr>
<td valign="top">

3. Keep the Word Help window on top of the open Word window.

</td>
<td valign="top">

a. On the title bar, **click the Restore Down button**  to restore the Help window.

b. In the Word Help window, in the Word Help toolbar, **place the mouse pointer over the Keep On Top button** to view the ScreenTip.

c. **Click the Keep On Top button.**

d. To verify that the Word Help window stays on top, **click anywhere in the Word window.**

e. **Close the Word Help window.**

</td>
</tr>
</table>

TOPIC E
Enter Text

In the first few topics in this lesson, you identified the user interface elements in Word and arranged the Word environment to suit your needs. With your working environment organized, you are now ready to begin basic document editing. In this topic, you will start to create a basic Word document by entering text.

Word is a powerful word processor. However, with no words to process, the program does little more than take up room on your computer. The first step toward creating a document is to capture your ideas in a form that Word can use, which is by entering text into an open document.

Default Typing Options

When you begin typing in a new blank document, certain things will happen automatically to help you enter text neatly, quickly, and accurately.

- The *word wrap* function will automatically continue a long line of text at the beginning of the next line so that you can continue typing. There is no need to manually end each line of text by pressing Enter when you get close to the right margin.

- *AutoCorrect* fixes common typographical errors, misspelled words, and incorrect capitalization.

- The Check Spelling And Grammar As You Type feature displays a wavy red or wavy green underline below text that Word considers either a spelling or grammar mistake, respectively. You can right-click the underlined item and Word will suggest corrections for you.

- *Smart tags* are hidden tags that are represented by a button that is displayed in response to a given action. Clicking a smart tag displays a list of options related to the action performed.

The AutoCorrect Options Button

The AutoCorrect Options button is a hidden tag that appears below the word or the capitalized letter that has been modified using the AutoCorrect feature. This button provides options to undo automatic corrections, stop particular automatic corrections, or control AutoCorrect options by using the AutoCorrect dialog box.

Formatting Marks

Definition:

Formatting marks are non-printing document indicators that appear in the text area to indicate the location of spaces, paragraphs, tabs, line breaks, and so on. By clicking the Show/Hide button on the Home tab, you can turn the formatting marks on or off.

Example:

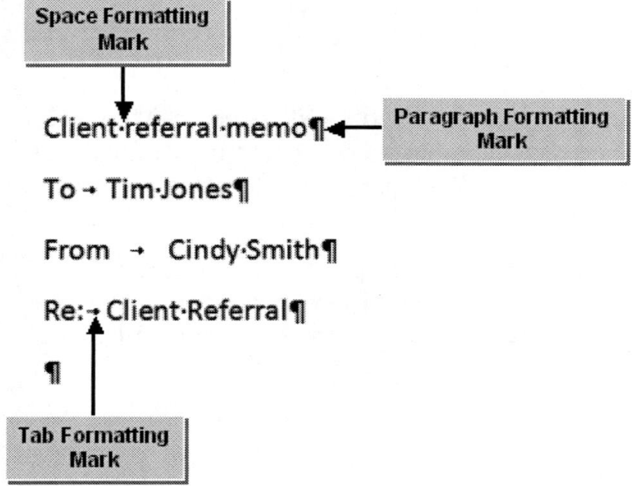

Figure 1-7: *Different formatting marks in Word.*

How to Enter Text

Procedure Reference: Create a Blank Document and Enter Text

To create a blank document and enter text:

1. Click the Office button and choose New.
2. In the New Document dialog box, in the Blank And Recent section, select Blank Document.
3. Click Create.
4. In the Word document, position the insertion point at the location where you want to enter text.
5. Type the desired text.
6. If necessary, press Enter to end a paragraph or to create a blank line between paragraphs.
7. If necessary, on the Home tab of the Ribbon, in the Paragraph group, click the Show/Hide button to display the formatting marks.
8. If you need to delete a character or space, position the insertion point before or after the character to be deleted, and press Backspace to delete one character to the left and Delete to delete one character to the right.
9. If you would like to delete a blank line, position the mouse pointer at the beginning of the blank line and press Delete.

ACTIVITY 1-5

Entering Text in a Document

Scenario:

You work for a real estate company named Burke Properties. You took a phone message for a client named Ms. Ellen Thomas. The client is available for a meeting on the first of next month to discuss buying the Schyler house on Elm Street. Since this location is outside your sales territory, you need to draft a client referral memo in Word to pass the information about the client to the appropriate agent, Tim Jones.

What You Do	How You Do It
1. Create a new blank document.	a. **Click the Office button and choose New.**
	b. In the New Document dialog box, in the Blank And Recent section, **verify that Blank Document is selected and click Create.**
2. Type the memo's heading information.	a. On the Home tab of the Ribbon, in the Paragraph group, **click the Show/Hide button ¶** to turn on the formatting marks.
	b. **Type *Client Referral Memo* and press Enter** to end the line.
	c. A paragraph mark appears where you ended the line. **Press Enter** to add a blank line.
	d. **Type *To:* and press Tab.**
	e. The tab character appears as an arrow. **Type *Tim Jones* and press Enter.**
	f. **Type *From:* and press Tab.**
	g. **Type your first and last name and press Enter.**
	h. **Type *Re:* and press Tab.**
	i. **Type *Client Help***

3. **Replace the word "Help" with "Referral".**

   a. With the insertion point after the word Help, **press Backspace four times** to delete the word.

   b. **Type *Referral* and press Enter.**

4. **Type the memo's first sentence.**

   a. **Press Enter** to add a blank line after the reference line.

   b. **Type *Ms. Ellen Thomas wants to see the Schyler house in your territory***

   c. A wavy line appears under "Schyler" because the Check Spelling feature is active and this is not a common dictionary word. **Press Spacebar and type *(the one on Elm Street).*** to conclude the sentence.

5. **Check the functionality of the AutoCorrect feature.**

   a. To start the next sentence, **press the Spacebar and type *teh***

   b. **Press Spacebar** to automatically correct the word.

   c. **Move the mouse pointer just below the word "The"** to display the AutoCorrect Options button.

   d. **Click the AutoCorrect Options button.**

   e. From the AutoCorrect Options drop-down list, **select Control AutoCorrect Options.**

   f. In the AutoCorrect dialog box, **scroll in the AutoCorrect settings list** to verify that there is a setting to convert "teh" to "the."

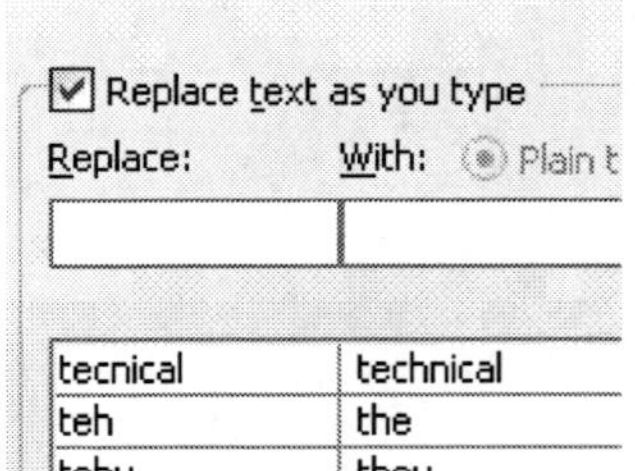

   g. **Click Cancel** to close the dialog box.

6. Finish the memo.

a. **Verify that the insertion point is after the space after the word "The" and type *first of next month is a good meeting time. Call me for details.***

b. As you type, the text wraps automatically at the right edge of the document. **Press Enter** to end the paragraph.

You do not need to close the document. You can use the same file for the next activity.

TOPIC F

Save a Document

You have entered text in a document. You may want to save this document for future reference. In this topic, you will save a document.

Working on an important document for hours would be a waste if we are unable to retrieve this information to use it later. Thus, it is necessary to save the document.

Word 2007 File Types

All Word 2007 files use Extensible Markup Language (XML) as the basic file format. The Word XML format is a compact, robust file format that enables easy integration of Word documents into other applications and platforms. Word 2007 supports a number of other file types as well.

Other Word File Formats

The following table lists some of the important file formats you can use in Word 2007.

File Type	Description
.docx	This is the default type in which all Word 2007 documents are saved.
.docm	This is a basic XML file type that can store VBA macrocode. Macros are sets of Word commands and instructions grouped together as a single command and a VBA helps us to modify these macros.
.doc	The Word 97–2003 Document (*.doc) option is used to save the document in a format compatible with many previous versions of Word.
	The Word 97–2003 & 6.0/95–RTF (*.doc) option is used to save a Word document in the format compatible with Word 95 with Rich Text Format.
.dotx/.dotm	.dotx is the default type for a Word template. It is used while saving document styles and formatting.
	.dotm is the default type for a Word macro-enabled template. Microsoft Office Word 2007 stores macro code for use with other Word documents. By default, documents are saved as .docx files even when created from a Office Word 2007 XML Macro-Enabled Template.
.dot	This file type enables you to save a Word template in the Word 97 through Word 2003 versions.
.pdf	This file type enables you to save the Word document as an Adobe PDF (Portable Document Format) file.
.htm or .html	This file type saves the Word document as a web page. This renders the document's contents non-editable.
	Saving the Word document as a filtered web page will remove Office-specific tags and also disable a few of the Word features.
.rtf	This is a common file type which enables you to save any text document with formatting.
.txt	This file type is used to save documents without any text formatting.
.xml	This file type is used to save the document as a Word XML document and is very similar to the basic *.html file type.

Advantages of the XML File Format

Previous versions of Word used the .doc file format by default. The XML file format provides several improvements to the .doc file format that are very useful for end users.

Feature	Advantage
Smaller file size	The new format uses zip compression to reduce file size by as much as 75 percent. These new file formats reduce the disk space required to store files and the bandwidth used to share documents across networks.
Improved information recovery	The files saved in these new formats are structured modularly. Different data components in the file are stored separately. Therefore, the file can be opened even if a component within the file is damaged or corrupted.
Easier detection of documents with macros	The new file formats with their distinct file name extensions make it easy to distinguish files that contain macros from those that don't. File extensions ending with x cannot contain VBA macros or ActiveX controls, whereas files ending with m can.
Easy integration and interoperability of information	Information created within the Office applications can be easily used by other business applications.

The Save Command

The Save command is used to save a newly created document or to save the changes you make to an existing document. While saving a file for the first time, the Save As dialog box is displayed, which prompts the user to type a name for the file and to specify the location in which the file needs to be saved. By default, a Word document is saved with the .docx file extension.

The Save As Command

The Save As command on the Office button is used to save an existing document with a new file name, with a new file extension, or in a new location. It also provides direct access to options that enable you to save a copy of the file in the default Word 2007 file format, as a template, in the Word 97-2003 file format, and also to publish a copy of the file as a PDF or XPS file.

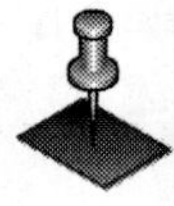

PDF (Portable Document Format) and XPS (XML paper Specification) are document formats that integrate creating a document and its viewing on the window. To save in either of these formats you will need to install an add-in program from Microsoft; see the Word Help system for more information.

Save vs. Save As

The Save command saves an existing document with the same name in the same location, whereas the Save As command enables you to change the name of the file, the location in which the file need to be stored, or the type of the file.

Compatibility with Other Word Formats

If you share information with users of earlier versions of Word, there are various tools you can use to ensure that the different document formats are compatible.

Compatibility Method	Description
Convert a document	You can use the Convert option to convert a document saved in an earlier version of Word to the Word 2007 file format. Click the Office button and choose Convert.
Save as an earlier version	You can save a .docx document in a file format compatible with earlier versions of Word. In the Save As dialog box, select the document type for the appropriate version of Word from the Save As dialog box. The *Compatibility Checker* will run to inform you if there are any features in the current .docx document that will not be preserved in the earlier file format. For example, some new text or graphic effects might be combined into a single object in the earlier file version.
Check compatibility manually	To run the Compatibility Checker manually, click the Office button and choose Prepare→Run Compatibility Checker. The Compatibility Checker will tell you if there are any compatibility issues or not.

How to Save a Document

Procedure Reference: Save a Document with the Save As Command

To use the Save As command to save a document for the first time or to save a copy of a document with a different file name or location:

1. Click the Office button and choose Save As to display the Save As dialog box.

The first time you save a new document, the Save As dialog box will also open if you choose Save, click the Save button, or press Ctrl + S.

2. In the Save As dialog box, click the Save In drop-down arrow and navigate to the location where you want to save the document.

3. If necessary, from the Save As Type drop-down list, select the desired format to select a different file format.

4. In the File Name text box, type the name of the file.

5. Click Save.

Procedure Reference: Use the Save Command to Save Changes to an Existing Document

To save changes made to an existing document:

1. Open and modify the document.

2. Save the changes.
   - Click the Office button and choose Save.
   - On the Quick Access toolbar, click the Save button.
   - Or, press Ctrl+S.

ACTIVITY 1-6

Saving a Document

Before You Begin:
The Client Referral Memo document is open.

Scenario:
After you have finished typing the client referral memo, you wish to maintain a copy of it for your own reference. Your agent, Tim Jones, has only Word 2003 installed on his computer, and therefore, you need to create a copy of the document for him in the Word 2003 file format.

What You Do	How You Do It
1. Save the document.	a. With the Client Referral Memo open, **click the Office button and choose Save As.**
	b. In the Save As dialog box, **navigate to C:\084893Data\Creating a Basic Document.**
	c. In the File Name text box and Save As Type text box, **verify that Client Referral Memo.docx is the file name and Word Document (*.docx) is the Save As Type. Click Save.**

File <u>n</u>ame:	Client Referral Memo.docx
Save as <u>t</u>ype:	Word Document (*.docx)

2. Check the compatibility of the memo with the 2003 version of the Word application.	a. **Click the Office button and choose Prepare→Run Compatibility Checker.**
	b. **Verify that there are no compatibility issues and click OK.**

<table>
<tr><td>3.</td><td>Save a copy of the file on the Desktop in the Word 2003 file format.</td><td>a.</td><td>Click the Office button and choose Save As→Word 97-2003 Document.</td></tr>
<tr><td></td><td></td><td>b.</td><td>In the Save As dialog box, in left pane, click Desktop.</td></tr>
<tr><td></td><td></td><td>c.</td><td>Verify that the Save As Type is Word 97–2003 Document (*.doc) and click Save.</td></tr>
<tr><td></td><td></td><td>d.</td><td>Close the document.</td></tr>
</table>

TOPIC G
Preview and Print a Document

You have saved your work in a document and are now ready to print it. Before you print the document, it is smart to preview the document so you can see what it might look like when printed. In this topic, you will preview and print your document.

Whether you realize it or not, printing a document costs money. Each page may cost only a few cents for paper and ink, but those pennies add up quickly if you are repeatedly printing a multi-page document, just to see how it will look on paper or to do a quick hard copy edit. By previewing your document before printing, you can still see how it will look and identify obvious errors without wasting money and the time it takes to print additional copies.

Print Preview

Print Preview is a view mode that enables you to view a document as it would appear on paper when printed. You can view or modify the document in this view to suit your requirements. You can access Print Preview from the Print selection on the Office button.

Print Preview Options

When a document is displayed in the Print Preview mode, the Print Preview tab contains several groups that provide options to print a document with desired settings.

Print Preview Group	*Options in This Group*
Print	The Print group enables you to print the document or set print or display options.
Page Setup	The Page Setup group enables you to adjust printed margins, change the print orientation between portrait (vertical) or landscape (horizontal), or select a different paper size.
Zoom	The Zoom group enables you to control the print preview appearance in various ways such as previewing the document at a particular percentage of its actual size, or by previewing one or two pages at a time.
Preview	The Preview group enables you to change options for the Print Preview mode. For example, you can show or hide the ruler tools that measure your document horizontally or vertically. You can also use buttons in the preview group for navigating from page to page within Print Preview.

The Print Dialog Box

The most common options in the Print dialog box enable users to print documents with the desired settings.

For information on other options in the Print dialog box, see Microsoft Office Word Help.

Common Print Option	Description
Name	Displays the name of the printer in use.
Properties	Displays the printer's Properties dialog box. This option allows you to modify the layout of the page to be printed.
Page Range	Enables you to print the whole document, just the current page, or a range of pages.
Copies	Enables you to specify the number of copies of document you want to print.
Collate	Arranges each copy in sequential order when you need to print more than one copy of the same document.
Print What	Allows you to print the document itself or other attributes of the document such as its properties.
Print	Allows you to select and print odd pages, even pages, or all pages in the specified page range.
Zoom	Allows you to specify the number of pages to print on a single sheet of paper and their scaling.
Options	Opens the Display tab in the Word Options dialog box. The Display tab enables you to further modify the appearance of the content on screen and on print mode.

How to Preview and Print a Document

Procedure Reference: Preview a Document

To preview a document:

1. Click the Office button and choose Print→Print Preview, or press Ctrl+F2.

2. Use the tools in the Zoom group and on the Microsoft Office Status Bar, to view the document at the desired magnification level. For example, you can specify a percentage of actual size, click buttons to preview one or two pages at once, or click Zoom to open the Zoom dialog box and select additional options.

 Clicking the Magnifier mouse pointer at a particular region of the document would magnify that region of the document to 100 percent. Clicking the magnifier again will undo the change in magnification.

3. To navigate through the previewed document, click the Next Page or Previous Page buttons in the Zoom group.

4. To make changes to the document, uncheck the Magnifier check box in the Preview group; the mouse pointer will change to an I-beam and you will be able to edit the document. Check the Magnifier check box when you are done with editing.

5. Click Close Print Preview in the Preview group or press Esc to return to the original document view.

Procedure Reference: Print a Document

To print a document:

1. Display the Print dialog box.
   - On the Office button, click Print.
   - On the Quick Access toolbar, click the Print button.
   - On the Print Preview tab, click the Print button.
   - Or, press Ctrl+P.

2. In the Print dialog box, in the Printer section, set the printer options.

3. In the Page Range section, set the page range to be printed: All, Current Page, or a specified range of pages.

4. In the Copies section, in the Number Of Copies text box, type the number of copies that you want to print. If you print multiple copies, check the Collate check box to arrange the multiple copies of the printed document in sequential order.

5. If necessary, set Zoom or other print options.

6. Click OK to print the document with the specified settings.

ACTIVITY 1-7

Previewing and Printing a Document

Data Files:

About Us.docx

Conditions:

A print driver is installed on your computer.

Scenario:

You have been asked to provide a printed copy of the document that you have created to provide a company overview to new employees. Before printing, you want to preview the document to verify whether the document looks as desired.

What You Do	How You Do It
1. Open the About Us document from the Recent Documents list.	a. Click the Office button.
	b. In the Recent Documents list, **select About Us.docx.**
2. Preview the document at different zoom levels.	a. **Click the Office button and choose Print→Print Preview.**
	b. In Print Preview mode, the mouse pointer appears as a magnifying glass. On the Print Preview tab, in the Zoom group, **click the Zoom button.**
	c. In the Zoom dialog box, in the Zoom To section, **select the 75% option and click OK.**
	d. The zoom value appears on the Microsoft Office Status Bar. On the Status Bar, **click the Zoom In button** to increase the magnification to 80 percent.
	e. **Click the Zoom In button three times** to increase the magnification to 110%.

3. View both pages of the document.

   a. In the Preview group, **click Next Page** to view the next page of the document.

   b. In the Zoom group, **click Two Pages** to view both pages of the document simultaneously.

   c. In the Preview group, **click the Close Print Preview button** to switch to the document view mode.

4. Print two copies of the entire document.

   a. **Click the Office button and choose Print→Print.**

   b. In the Copies section, in the Number Of Copies text box, **type 2**

   c. **Verify that the Collate check box is checked and click OK** to print the document.

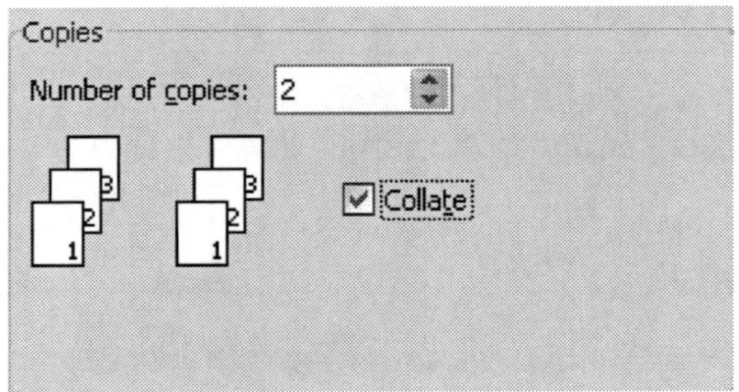

5. Print a copy of the "Our Goals" page.

   a. **Click the Office button and choose Print→Print.**

   b. **Verify that the number of copies is set to 1.**

   c. The "Our Goals" page is the second page in the document. In the Page Range section, **select Pages.** In the Pages text box, **type 2**

   d. **Click OK** to print only the second page.

   e. **Close the document.**

Lesson 1 Follow-up

In this lesson, you created a document by entering text, saving, and printing the document. Not only are you now ready not only to produce your own simple documents, but you will also use these fundamental skills to create more complex documents with Microsoft Word.

1. **What do you think about Word's default typing options? Do you think they're useful or distracting?**

2. **How does customizing the Quick Access toolbar help you in your work?**

2 | Editing a Document

Lesson Time: 60 minutes

Lesson Objectives:

In this lesson, you will edit documents by locating and modifying text.

You will:

- Navigate and select text in a document.

- Insert, delete, or rearrange text in an existing document.

- Undo or redo changes made to a document.

- Find and replace text.

Introduction

In the previous lesson, you created a basic document. Once you have created the basic structure of documents, you will often choose to perform additional editing of the text. In this lesson, you will edit documents.

Editing a handwritten document requires you to rewrite the entire document to include the changes. Word minimizes the effort required to revise your documents by enabling you to change your existing documents any time, without using messy correction fluid or having to start your document over again.

TOPIC A

Navigate and Select Text in a Document

In this lesson, you will edit documents. Most document editing techniques require you to navigate to a desired location and select text in a document. In this topic, you will navigate and select text within a document.

The two basic components that allow you to thoroughly view the different sections in a document are the keyboard and mouse. In order to navigate in a document, though, it is very important to quickly decide on the component that best suits the situation. Using the most appropriate navigation technique in a document may save you a lot of navigation time.

Scroll Bars

In addition to using keyboard techniques to navigate, you can use Word's two scroll bars to move up, down, left, or right in a document. When you navigate with the scroll bars, the location of the insertion point does not change. Use the vertical scroll bar, located at the extreme right side of the application window, to scroll up or down. Use the horizontal scroll bar, just above the Microsoft Office Status Bar, to scroll left or right. The scroll arrows at the extreme ends of the scroll bars allow the user to scroll a document slowly. The scroll boxes between the scroll arrows can be dragged with the mouse to enable the user to quickly scroll through a document.

 The left corner of the Microsoft Office Status Bar always shows the insertion point's current location.

The Next and Previous Buttons

In addition to the scroll bar components, you can also use the Next and Previous buttons to navigate through a document. These buttons are located below the vertical scroll bar in the Word environment. The Next and Previous buttons are part of the Object Browser, which contains the options to browse through the different parts of a document. By default, the Object Browser is configured in such a way that you can use the Next and the Previous buttons to browse by page. You can also customize the Object Browser to navigate to a specific location, such as a line, heading, table, or graphic in a document.

The Selection Bar

Selection bar is the area at the left margin of a document that is used to select text. When positioned on the selection bar, the mouse pointer will change from an I-beam to a right-pointing arrow. On the selection bar, you can click to select a line, double-click to select a paragraph, or triple-click to select the entire document.

The Mini Toolbar

Whenever you make a text selection in a document, the *Mini toolbar* appears above the selected text. You can use commands on the Mini toolbar to format text without having to move to the Ribbon. This toolbar disappears when you move the mouse pointer away from the selection. You can also invoke the Mini toolbar along with a list of commands by right-clicking anywhere in the document.

How to Navigate and Select Text in a Document

Procedure Reference: Navigate and Select Text in a Document

To navigate and select text in a document:

1. Open the document.
2. Use the appropriate navigation techniques to move to the desired location.
3. Use the appropriate selection methods to select the text.

Keyboard Navigation Techniques

The navigation keys on the keyboard allow users to easily navigate within a document.

Pressing This Key/ Keys	Moves the Insertion Point To This Position
Right arrow or Left arrow	One space to the right or left.
Ctrl+Right arrow or Ctrl+Left arrow	One word to the right or left.
Down arrow or Up arrow	One line down or up.
Ctrl+Down arrow or Ctrl+Up arrow	One paragraph down or up.
Page Down or Page Up	One screen down or up.
Ctrl+Page Down or Ctrl+ Page Up	Beginning of the next page or the beginning of the previous page.
Home or End	Beginning or end of a line.
Ctrl+Home or Ctrl+End	Beginning or end of the document.

Scroll Bar Navigation Techniques

You can use the vertical and horizontal scroll bars to navigate quickly to different parts of the document without changing the position of the insertion point.

If You Need To	Do This
Scroll up or down one line at a time	On the vertical scroll bar, click the scroll up arrow or the scroll down arrow.
Scroll up or down multiple lines	On the vertical scroll bar, click above or below the scroll box.
Scroll left or right	On the horizontal scroll bar, click the scroll left arrow or the scroll right arrow.

If You Need To	**Do This**
Display the top, bottom, or center of a document	On the vertical scroll bar, drag the scroll box to the top, bottom, or center of the scroll bar.

Text Selection Methods

In a document, you can select individual characters, words, sentences, paragraphs, or even the entire document using the mouse, keyboard, or a combination of both.

To Select This	**Do This**
Variable amounts of text	• Click and drag the mouse to select a block of text. • Place the insertion point at the beginning of the text, hold down the Shift key, and press an arrow key to extend the selection in the desired direction. • Place the insertion point at the beginning of the text, hold down the Shift key, and click at the end of the desired block of text.
A word	Double-click the word. This selects the trailing space after the word, but does not select punctuation.
A line or lines of text	Click in the selection bar to the left of the line. To select multiple contiguous lines, click and drag in the selection bar.
A sentence	Hold Ctrl and click anywhere in the sentence. This selects the sentence and its closing punctuation.
A paragraph	Triple-click in the paragraph or double-click in the selection bar next to the paragraph.
Noncontiguous sections	To select items that are not adjacent, select the first item, line, or paragraph, and then hold down Ctrl while you select additional items.
The entire document	• Triple-click the selection bar. • Press Ctrl+A. • Or, on the Home tab, in the Editing group, from the Select drop-down list, select Select All.
Deselect text	Make another selection or click anywhere in the text area away from the selected text.

ACTIVITY 2-1

Navigating and Selecting Text in a Document

Data Files:

Burke Draft.docx

Before You Begin:

From the C:\084893Data\Editing a Document folder, open Burke Draft.docx.

Scenario:

You need to attend an important client meeting the next day. The details about the client are captured in the Burke Draft.docx file. This information will be very helpful for you during the client meeting, so you need to review the document to familiarize yourself with the content.

What You Do	**How You Do It**
1. **Display different parts of the document using the vertical scroll bar.**	a. On the vertical scroll bar, **click the scroll down arrow,** to view the text.
	b. **Click the scroll bar area below the scroll box** to scroll one screen at a time.
	c. Although you are scrolling, the insertion point remains at the top of the document. **Click the Next Page button,** to move the insertion point to the top of the next page.
	d. On the vertical scroll bar, **click and drag the scroll box to the bottom of the scroll bar.**

As you drag the scroll box, you may notice a ScreenTip with the number of the current page being displayed.

e. **Drag the scroll box to the top of page 2 of the document.**

2. Move the insertion point to different parts of the document.

a. If necessary, on page 2, **click at the beginning of the first paragraph.**

b. **Press the Right arrow key** to move the insertion point one character to the right.

c. **Press the Left arrow key** to move the insertion point one character to the left.

d. **Press the Up and Down arrow keys and the Page Up and Page Down keys** to move to various document locations.

e. **Press Ctrl+End** to move the insertion point to the end of the document.

3. Select various sections of text.

a. **Return to the beginning of the document.**

b. At the beginning of the document, **click and drag until the end of the text "SECOND DRAFT"** to select it.

c. To select the line that begins with the text "Burke Properties was founded," **move the mouse pointer on the Selection bar until the shape of the mouse pointer changes to a right-pointing arrow and click.**

d. To extend the selection to include the word "firm," **hold down Shift and press the Right Arrow key five times.**

e. To select the paragraph below "About Us," **triple-click the paragraph.**

4. Select the entire Word document.

a. On the Home tab, in the Editing group, **click Select and choose Select All.**

b. **Click anywhere in the text area** to deselect the text.

c. **Close Burke Draft.docx.**

TOPIC B

Insert, Delete, or Rearrange Text

In the previous topic, you navigated within a document and selected document text. You can use these basic navigation and selection skills to insert, delete, or rearrange text as needed. In this topic, you will insert, delete, and rearrange text.

You want the content in your document to be as clear as possible. That's not always the case after typing a first draft. As you enter text, you often type the words as they crystallize in your thoughts. Once you've reviewed a document, chances are that you will want to add or delete text or rearrange existing text to clarify the message you are trying to convey.

The Clipboard Group

The *Clipboard group* on the Home tab gives you access to the Clipboard, a temporary holding area for information that you want to move or copy to other locations. You can use the Clipboard group to move or copy text and associated text styles to the Clipboard, to paste text from the Clipboard to other locations, or to set Clipboard options.

Text Moving and Copying Options

Text or a selection of text can be moved from one location to another within or between documents.

Method	Description
Cut and paste	After selecting text, you can move it to the Clipboard, and then paste it in the desired location. You can move text to the Clipboard by using the Clipboard group, the shortcut menu, or the Ctrl+X keyboard shortcut.
Drag	After selecting text, it can be moved from the current location by directly dragging it to the desired location. When you drag text, it is not placed on the Clipboard.
Copy and paste	After selecting text, you can copy it to the Clipboard, and then paste it into the desired location. You can copy text to the Clipboard by using the Clipboard group, the shortcut menu, or the Ctrl+C keyboard shortcut.

Text Pasting Options

Any text or sections of text that have been copied or cut can be pasted in any part of the document using the Paste options in the Clipboard group.

Option	Description
Paste	Pastes the copied or cut item in the desired location.
Paste Special	Opens the Paste Special dialog box, where you can specify the format in which the selected item should appear when pasted.

Option	Description
Paste as Hyperlink	Pastes the text as a hyperlink so that when you hold down Ctrl and click a pasted item, it takes you to the location from where the item has been copied or cut.

The Paste Options Smart Tag

When you paste an item, the Paste Options Smart Tag is displayed immediately next to the pasted item. This tag holds a list of options that enable users to specify the formatting for the pasted item. You can retain the source formatting of the item; change the formatting of the item so that it matches the text in the destination; paste the text only; or customize cut, copy, and paste options.

The Clipboard Task Pane

The *Clipboard task pane* lists the objects that have been copied or cut from the document. You can use the Clipboard task pane to paste in all the Clipboard objects, clear the Clipboard, and to customize the task pane. Click the Clipboard Dialog Box Launcher button in the Clipboard group to open the Clipboard task pane.

Customization Options in the Clipboard Task Pane

The Clipboard task pane can be customized using the options available in the Options drop-down list.

Option	Description
Show Office Clipboard Automatically	Shows the Clipboard as soon as a document is opened.
Show Office Clipboard When Ctrl+C Is Pressed Twice	Shows the Clipboard when Ctrl+C is pressed two times.
Collect Without Showing Office Clipboard	Collects the items to the Clipboard without displaying the Clipboard task pane.
Show Office Clipboard Icon On Taskbar	Displays the Office Clipboard icon on the taskbar.
Show Status Near Taskbar When Copying	Displays the status of the task pane near the taskbar when an item is copied.

How to Insert, Delete, or Rearrange Text

Procedure Reference: Insert or Delete Text

To insert or delete text:

1. Place the insertion point where you want to insert the new text, or adjacent to the text you want to delete.
2. To insert new text, type the text.
3. To delete text, use the appropriate method.
    -   To delete characters to the left of the insertion point, press Backspace.
    -   To delete characters to the right of the insertion point, press Delete.
    -   To delete a block of text, select it and press Delete.

Procedure Reference: Move or Copy Text

To move or copy text to a new location:

1. Select the text you want to move or copy.
2. Cut or copy the selected text.
    -   On the Home tab, in the Clipboard group, click the Cut button or the Copy button.
    -   Press Ctrl+X to cut or Ctrl+C to copy.
    -   Or, right-click and choose Cut or Copy.
3. Place the insertion point at the location where you want to move or copy the text.
4. Paste the text.
    -   On the Home tab, in the Clipboard group, click the Paste button.
    -   Press Ctrl+V.
    -   Or, right-click and choose Paste.
5. To move or copy multiple text selections, cut or copy each selection to the Clipboard.
6. To paste in multiple selections, open the Clipboard task pane and make the appropriate choice.
    -   In the Click An Item To Paste section, select items one after the other to paste them to the specified location.
    -   Click Paste All to paste all the items in the clipboard to the specified location.

Moving or Copying Between Documents

You can use standard move and copy techniques between documents and within a document. To switch between open documents, you can use any of a number of techniques:

-   On the View tab, in the Window group, choose Switch Windows to display the list of documents that are open and to select the document you want to display.
-   Press Ctrl+F6 to switch between open Word documents.
-   Press Alt+Tab to switch between all open documents.
-   Click the appropriate button on the Windows Taskbar.

ACTIVITY 2-2

Inserting, Deleting, and Rearranging Text

Data Files:

Second Draft.docx, Nolan Letter.docx

Before You Begin:

From the C:\084893Data\Editing a Document folder, open Nolan Letter.docx and Second Draft.docx.

Scenario:

As you were reviewing the draft document, you noticed some text that seems out of place. On page one, you feel that the "Our Company Affiliations" heading and the paragraph that immediately follows it should be moved down in the document so that they precede the paragraph on page two that begins with "Buying a Home".

You also realize that some content is missing from the draft document; specifically, a list of things a realtor does for his or her clients under the "Selling Your Home" paragraph on page two and the Burke Properties guarantee on page three below the "Our Guarantee" paragraph. Fortunately, you recall seeing that information in a letter written to Beth Nolan.

What You Do	How You Do It
1. In the Second Draft document, **delete the first word in the title.**	a. If necessary, in the Second Draft document, **click at the beginning of the document, before the word "THE."**
	b. **Press Delete four times** to delete the word and the trailing space after it.
2. **Insert the word "real estate" into the second full sentence.**	a. In the sentence that begins with "We arrange", **click to place the insertion point at the beginning of the word "services"**
	b. **Type *real estate* and press Spacebar.**

<table>
<tr>
<td>

3. **Cut the heading "Our Company Affiliations," the text, and the blank line below it.**

</td>
<td>

a. In the middle of page 1, **select the "Our Company Affiliations" heading and paragraph and the paragraph formatting mark that follows.**

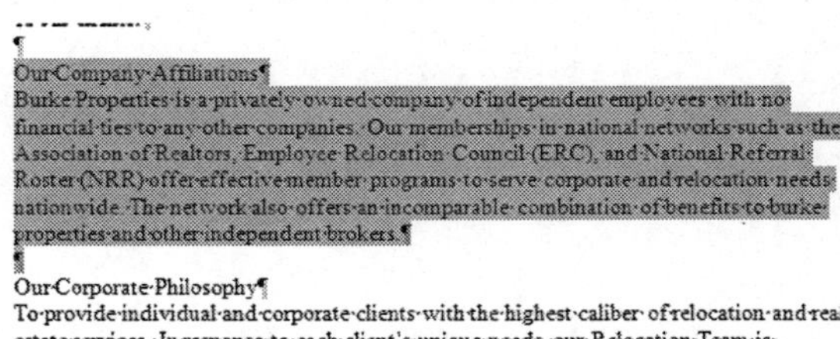

b. On the Home tab, in the Clipboard group, **click the Cut button.**

</td>
</tr>
<tr>
<td>

4. **Move the text to page two, before the "Buying a Home" heading.**

</td>
<td>

a. **Press Page Down twice** to navigate to the middle of the next page.

b. **Place the insertion point at the beginning of the Buying a Home heading.**

c. On the Home tab, in the Clipboard group, **click Paste.**

</td>
</tr>
<tr>
<td>

5. **Copy the necessary text from the Nolan Letter.docx file.**

</td>
<td>

a. **Click the Nolan Letter button on the Taskbar.**

b. On the Home tab, in the Clipboard group, **click the Dialog Box Launcher button** to display the Clipboard task pane.

c. In Nolan Letter.docx, **select the "Here's what a realtor" list along with the paragraph mark.**

d. On the Home tab, in the Clipboard group, **click the Copy button** to copy the selection.

e. **Press Page Down** to reach the end of the document.

f. In the last paragraph, after the text "P.S.", **select the entire sentence which begins with the text, "We are so sure", along with the paragraph mark.**

g. **Press Ctrl+C to copy the selection** and add it to the Clipboard task pane.

</td>
</tr>
</table>

6. **Use the Clipboard task pane to paste the first item of the copied text.**

   a. **Switch to the Second Draft document.**

   b. **Scroll to the bottom of page 1.**

   c. In the last paragraph, **place the insertion point in the blank line below the text, "Selling Your Home."**

   d. **Open the Clipboard task pane.**

   e. In the Clipboard task pane, in the Click An Item To Paste list box, **click the item that begins with the text, "Here's what a realtor"** to paste a copy of it into the document.

7. **Paste the next item of text.**

   a. **Press Ctrl+Page Down** to navigate to the next page.

   b. **Place the insertion point in the blank line below the "Our Guarantee" heading.**

   c. In the Clipboard task pane, in the Click An Item To Paste list box, **click the item that begins with the text, "We are so sure"** to paste a copy of it into the document.

   d. On the Clipboard task pane, **click Clear All** to clear all the items copied into the task pane.

8. **Save the document as *My Second Draft* and close the Nolan Letter document and the Clipboard task pane.**

   a. **Save the document as *My Second Draft.docx***

   b. **Close the Nolan Letter document.**

   c. On the top-right corner of the Clipboard task pane, **click the Close button** to close the task pane.

TOPIC C
Undo Changes

In the previous topic, you changed your document by inserting, deleting, or rearranging text. As you modify your document, it is typical to find that you make minor typographical errors, or otherwise make a change that you need to reverse. In this topic, you will undo document changes.

One of the great benefits of using computers to perform business tasks electronically instead of on paper is that you have the ability to reverse or revise the contents of documents easily, quickly, and neatly. In a paper document, it is very difficult to reverse a change and still preserve the professional look of the content. On a computer, however, it only takes a single click to reverse a change. Microsoft Word improves on this undo capability even further by enabling you to reverse or redo a series of changes and revert an open document back to any previous state that you choose.

Undo Options

The Undo options on the Quick Access toolbar help correct unnecessary or erroneous actions. You can undo an action by clicking the Undo button or by pressing Ctrl+Z. You can view the actions that you have performed earlier, listed in the reverse order, by clicking the drop-down list next to the Undo button. Deleted items, which are not collected by the Clipboard task pane, can be restored only by using the Undo command.

Redo Options

The Redo button on the Quick Access toolbar allows you to redo a series of actions in the reverse order that the changes were undone. The Redo option works only for the current working session. Once you close a document, the Redo list is cleared.

While you can undo or redo most actions, certain actions, such as opening, saving, or printing a document, cannot be undone. Only the actions that have been undone can be redone.

How to Undo or Redo Changes

Procedure Reference: Undo or Redo Actions

To undo or redo actions:

1. To undo an action, click the Undo button on the Quick Access toolbar or press Ctrl+Z.

2. To undo several actions, click the Undo drop-down arrow on the Quick Access toolbar to display the list of actions and select an option to undo the corresponding change, or press Ctrl+Z several times.

3. To redo an action, click the Redo button on the Quick Access toolbar or press Ctrl+Y.

4. To redo several actions, click the Redo button on the Quick Access toolbar several times, or press Ctrl+Y several times.

ACTIVITY 2-3
Recovering Deleted Blocks of Text

Before You Begin:
My Second Draft.docx is open.

Scenario:
You heard that the Kentucky, Ohio, and Texas offices were going to be closed soon, so you decide to delete those items from the Burke Properties Locations list. Before you complete editing the document, you realize that what you heard about the offices was a miscommunication. You decide to restore those three blocks of text to the list of offices once again.

What You Do	**How You Do It**
1. Delete the unnecessary text.	a. **Press Ctrl+End** to navigate to the end of the document.
	b. **Press Page Up twice** to display "Kentucky."
	c. **Select the Kentucky and Lexington paragraphs and the blank line following them.**

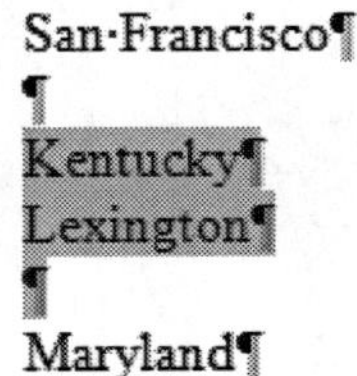

	d. **Press Delete** to delete the selection.
	e. **Select and delete the Ohio, Cleveland, and Toledo paragraphs and the blank line following them.**

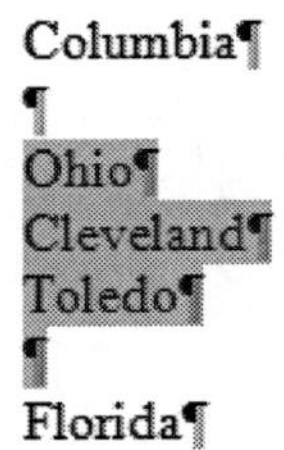

	f. **Select and delete the Texas, Dallas, and San Antonio paragraphs.**

2.   Undo the deletions.

a. On the Quick Access toolbar, **click the Undo button** to restore the Texas, Dallas, and San Antonio deletion.

b. **Click the Undo drop-down arrow** to display the drop-down list.

c. **Move the mouse pointer over the second Clear action** to highlight both Clear actions.

d. **Click the second Clear action** to restore both the Ohio and the Kentucky text blocks.

e. **Scroll up** to verify that the "Ohio" and the "Kentucky" text blocks have been restored.

f. **Save the file as *My New Draft.docx***

TOPIC D
Search and Replace Text

In the previous topic, you used Undo to reverse changes in a document. Another technique you can use to make changes throughout a document is to search for and replace specified text. In this topic, you will search for and replace text quickly and efficiently.

If you are working on a short document, it's not difficult to find the text you are looking for by scrolling up and down. However, if you are looking for a client's name in a multi-page legal document, that method is like looking for a needle in a haystack. It could take hours to find all the occurrences of the client's name and, in the end, you may miss one or two occurrences of the name anyway. Word enables you to locate every occurrence of the text you want to find and presents you with the opportunity to selectively replace an occurrence or replace all of them with the click of a button.

The Find And Replace Dialog Box

Clicking any of the Find, Replace, or Go To commands in the Editing group of the Home tab opens the corresponding tab in the Find And Replace dialog box.

Tab	Description
Find	Provides various Find options that will help you specify the search criteria. The keyboard shortcut, Ctrl+F, directly opens the Find tab in the Find And Replace dialog box.
Replace	Provides options to replace the found text with a different text. The keyboard shortcut, Ctrl+H, directly opens the Replace tab in the Find And Replace dialog box.
Go To	Provides options that let you specify where exactly you want to navigate. The keyboard shortcut, Ctrl+G, directly opens the Go To tab in the Find And Replace dialog box.

Find Options

The Find tab in the Find And Replace dialog box has various find options that will help you specify the search criteria.

Option	Used to
Find What	Specifies the text to be located. You can use wildcard characters to expand the search.
More	Displays the advanced find options to customize your search. For example, you can specify whether to search up or down, whether or not to match uppercase or lowercase, to find whole words or sections of words, to include or ignore punctuation or white space, or to search for formatting.
Reading Highlight	Highlights all the instances of the search criteria in the document.

Option	Used to
Find In	Locates every instance of the search criteria in the document.
Find Next	Locates the next instance of the search criteria in the document.
Cancel	Closes the Find And Replace dialog box.

Replace Options

The Replace tab in the Find And Replace dialog box contains options to replace the found text with a different text.

Option	Used To
Find What	Specifies the text to be located.
Replace With	Specifies the text with which the located data should be replaced.
More	Displays the advanced find options. These options will allow you to customize your search.
Replace	Replaces the selected instance of the search criteria with the new data.
Replace All	Replaces every instance of the search criteria with the new data.
Find Next	Locates the next instance of the search criteria in the document.
Cancel	Closes the Find And Replace dialog box.

Go To Options

The Go To tab in the Find And Replace dialog box contains options that allow you to specify exactly where you want to navigate to. In the Go To What list box, you can select an option to specify the exact location. For example, if you need to navigate to page two in a document, you can select Page, type the number 2, and click Go To. You can also navigate to the previous or next page by clicking the respective buttons on the tab.

How to Find and Replace Text

Procedure Reference: Find or Replace Text

To find or replace text in your document:

1. To open the Find And Replace dialog box, either click Find in the Editing group or press Ctrl+F.
2. In the Find What text box, type the text you want to locate. Include any special characters, such as tabs or double spaces.
3. If necessary, from the Reading Highlight drop-down list, select Highlight All to highlight all the instances of the search criteria in the document.
4. If necessary, click the More button to set advanced search options.
5. If necessary, click the Less button to hide the advanced search options.
6. Click Find Next to locate the first occurrence of the text in the document. Continue clicking Find Next to advance to the next occurrence.
7. To replace text that you find, click the Replace tab.
8. In the Replace With text box, type the text that you want to substitute for found occurrences. Include any special characters, such as tabs or double spaces.

 To display the Replace tab in the Find And Replace dialog box directly, either click Replace in the Editing group or press Ctrl+H.

9. Click Find Next to begin the search.
10. Make the appropriate selection to replace each instance of the text.
    - Click Replace to replace the highlighted text and continue searching for the next occurrence.
    - Click Find Next to leave the highlighted text unchanged and continue searching for the next occurrence.
    - Click Replace All to replace all occurrences of the text at the same time.

 If you change your mind about a replace operation, click the Undo button on the Quick Access toolbar. If you used the Replace button, Word will undo the replacements one by one. If you used the Replace All button, Word will undo all of the replacements at the same time.

11. When Word has finished searching the document and you have made the necessary replacements, click OK in the Microsoft Office Word message box.
12. Close the Find And Replace dialog box.

Procedure Reference: Navigate in a Document Using the Go To Command

To navigate in a document using the Go To command:

1. In the Editing group, click Find and select the Go To tab, or press Ctrl+G.
2. In the Go To What list box, select the document component you want to go to, such as a page, section, or line.
3. Type the number or name of the component you want to go to and click Go To.

ACTIVITY 2-4

Finding and Replacing Text

Before You Begin:
My New Draft.docx is open.

Scenario:
During the previous review of the Burke Properties document, "Burke Properties" wasn't properly capitalized in all instances. The "B" in Burke and the "P" in Properties should always be capitalized. As part of a new Human Resource department initiative, many job titles have been updated. You have been asked to make sure that the job title "broker" is changed to "agent". You also noticed that a heading on page two needs to be modified.

What You Do	How You Do It
1. Search the document for any instances of "burke properties" in lowercase and highlight them.	a. **Place your insertion point at the beginning of the document.**

b. To open the Find And Replace dialog box, on the Home tab, in the Editing group, **click Find.**

c. In the Find What text box, **type *burke properties*** with all lowercase letters.

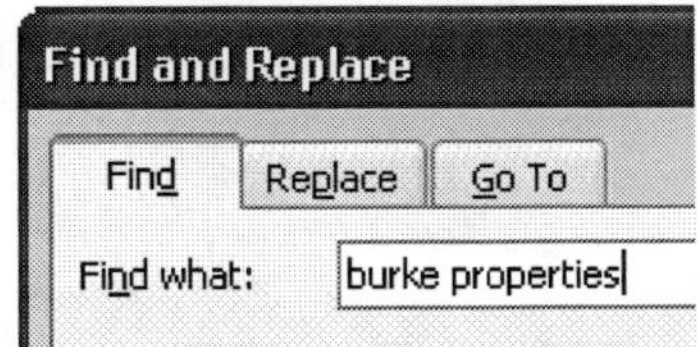

d. From the Reading Highlight drop-down list, **select Highlight All.**

e. All the instances of the text are highlighted. **Click the More button** to display the advanced search options.

f. In the Search Options section, **check the Match Case check box.**

g. **Click Less** to hide the advanced options in the dialog box.

2. **Initial case all instances of the text "burke properties".**	a. In the Find And Replace dialog box, **select the Replace tab** to display the replace options.
	b. **Click in the Replace With text box and type *Burke Properties***
	c. **Click Find Next** to find the first occurrence of "burke properties".

You can move the Find And Replace dialog box out of the way to see the found text in the document.

d. **Click Replace** to replace the lowercase instance with the uppercase version.

e. **Click Replace** to replace the next instance.

f. When Word has finished searching the document, in the Microsoft Office Word message box, **click OK.**

3. **Prepare to replace all instances of "broker" with "agent".**

    a. In the Find What text box, **type *broker***

    b. **Press Tab** to move the insertion point into the Replace With text box.

    c. **Type *agent***

    d. **Click More** to display the advanced search options.

    e. **Uncheck the Match Case check box.**

    f. **Click Less** to hide the advanced options in the dialog box.

4. **Find and replace the appropriate instances of the word "broker" with "agent".**

    a. **Click Find Next** to find the first occurrence of "broker".

    b. In the first occurrence, "broker" is part of the word "brokerage". **Click Find Next** to ignore that occurrence and to continue the search.

    c. In the next occurrence, **click Replace** to replace "broker" with "agent" and continue the search.

    d. **Click Replace to continue searching and replacing appropriate occurrences of "broker" with "agent".**

    e. When you have finished, in the Microsoft Office Word message box, **click OK** to end the search.

5. **Delete the incorrect word in page two of the document.**

    a. In the Find And Replace dialog box, **select the Go To tab** to display the Go To options.

    b. **Verify that the Page option is selected by default in the Go To What list box.**

    c. In the Enter Page Number text box, **type 2**

    d. **Click Go To** to move the insertion point to the beginning of second page.

    e. In the Find And Replace dialog box, **click Close** to close the dialog box.

f. In the heading "Special Network", **double-click the word "Special"** to select it and the space after it.

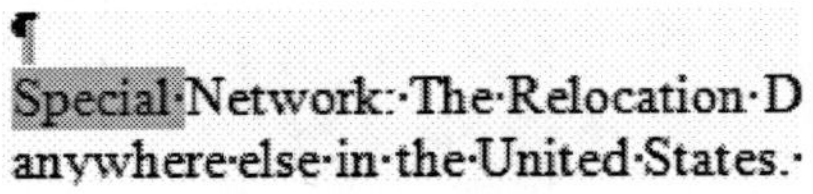

Special·Network:·The·Relocation·D anywhere·else·in·the·United·States.·

g. **Press Delete** to delete the selected text.

h. **Save the document as *My Burke Properties.docx* and close it.**

Lesson 2 Follow-up

In this lesson, you edited a document using a number of different editing techniques, such as moving and copying text, undoing changes, and replacing text. These basic editing skills will form the foundation of all the tasks you will perform in Microsoft Word documents.

1. **How do you currently edit documents?**

2. **How can the editing techniques in Word help you work more efficiently?**

3 | Formatting Text

Lesson Time: 30 minutes

Lesson Objectives:

In this lesson, you will format text.

You will:

- Change font appearance.
- Highlight text.

Introduction

Now that you have entered and edited text in a document, it is a good time to make that text more visually appealing. To make a selection stand out from the remaining text or meet a stylistic requirement, formatting is the solution to enhance your document. In this lesson, you will format text using the various options in Word 2007.

Whether you are designing a storybook for children or preparing a business report for your clients, you have to ensure that you hold the attention of your readers. In addition, you have to make sure that the readers don't lose out on any important information stated within the document. Word 2007, with its various font colors, sizes, and styles, can make any document attractive while ensuring that your reader is captivated by the information in your document.

TOPIC A

Change Font Appearance

In this lesson, you will format text. A fundamental aspect of the appearance of text is the appearance of the fonts you use to enter the text. In this topic, you will change font appearance.

While reading the newspaper or a magazine, your eyes automatically dart toward stories presented in varying fonts or sizes, or with other text enhancements and effects. These font appearance settings aid in drawing the attention of the audience, thereby helping them to focus on the important information in the document. Well-chosen font appearance options can enhance your message and help readers find the important information in the document.

Fonts

Definition:

A *font* is a predefined typeface with a unique design and character spacing. The set of characters in a font includes letters, numbers, and punctuation marks. A single document can use more than one font. You can modify the basic appearance of a font by using various formatting options. Word has a variety of built-in fonts that you can see on the Font group within the Home tab. The default font in Word is Calibri.

Example:

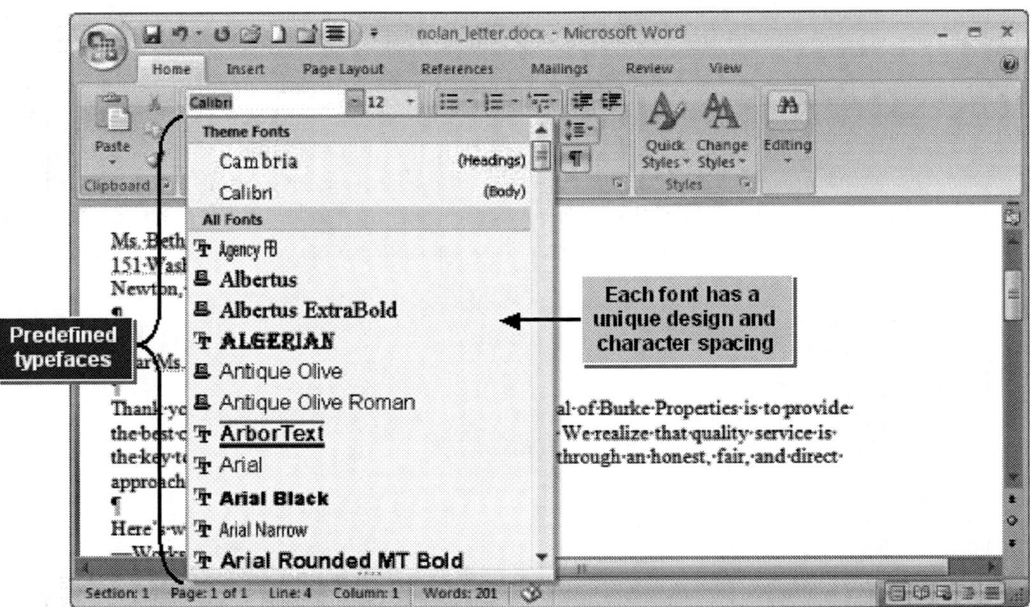

Figure 3-1: *The Font drop-down list with predefined typefaces.*

Font Size

In Word, font size is measured in points. One point equals 1/72 of an inch. Each font starts at a default point size, generally in the range of 10 to 12 points. You can change the font size for selected text by using the Mini toolbar or by using the Font Size Options in the Fonts group on the Home tab. You can also select a specific font size from the Font Size drop-down list in the Font group or the Font dialog box.

In the Font group, there are four options that affect the font size.

Option	Description
A˄	The Grow Font option increases the font size by one point each time you click it.
A˅	The Shrink Font option decreases the font size by one point each time you click it.
x₂	The Subscript option creates small letters and moves the text below the text baseline.
x²	The Superscript option creates small letters and moves the text above the text line.

Bold, Italic, and Underline

Three of the most common text-formatting options are bold, italic, and underline. Word enables you to apply any combination of these three options to selected text easily by using buttons in the Font group of the Home tab. You can also access these options from the Mini toolbar and in the Font dialog box.

Font Case

You can use the Change Case button in the Font group of the Home tab to apply different combinations of uppercase and lowercase fonts to document headings, subheadings, body text, and so on.

Font Case Option	Description
Sentence Case	Capitalizes the first letter of every sentence in the selected text.
Lowercase	Converts all the characters of the selected text into small letters.
Uppercase	Capitalizes all the characters of the selected text.
Capitalize Each Word	Capitalizes the first letter of each word in the selected text.
Toggle Case	Inverts the current capitalization of the selection. Lowercase letters become uppercase, and vice versa.

Font Effects

Effects are predefined text-enhancing options that emphasize text without affecting the typeface or the style of the text.

Effect	*Description*
Strikethrough	Runs a line through the selected text.
Double Strikethrough	Runs two lines through the selected text.
Superscript	Converts the text to small letters that appear above the text line.
Subscript	Converts the text to small letters that appear below the text baseline.
Shadow	Applies a shadow to each character of the selected text.
Outline	Applies an outline to each character of the selected text.
Emboss	Applies an etched impact on the text.
Engrave	Applies an embedded impact on the text.
Small Caps	Converts all the characters in the text to uppercase. However, the size of the first character of the word is larger than the rest of the letters.
All Caps	Capitalizes all the characters of the text, and all characters are the same size.
Hidden	Hides the content of the selected text.

Text Color

Adding color to your text helps in identifying important information in the document. You can use the Font Color button, the Font dialog box, or the Mini toolbar to change font color. The default text color is black, but you can change the color of selected text to any one of a palette of standard colors.

You can even mix your own custom font colors. For more information on custom colors, see Microsoft Office Word Help.

The Format Painter

The *Format Painter* is a formatting tool in the Clipboard group that allows you to duplicate the character or paragraph formatting in selected text and apply it to one or more additional selections. It is also used to apply some basic graphics formatting. The Format Painter does not provide any formatting options of its own.

How to Change Font Appearance

Procedure Reference: Change Font Appearance

To change the font appearance:

1. Select the text you want to change.

2. Apply a different font.
   - Change the font using the Font drop-down list.
     - On the Home tab of the Ribbon, in the Font group, from the Font drop-down list, select the desired font.
     - Or, on the Mini toolbar, from the Font drop-down list, select the desired font.
   - Change the font using the Font dialog box.
     a. On the Home tab, in the Font group, click the Dialog Box Launcher button, or press Ctrl+Shift+F.
     b. In the Font dialog box, in the Font list box, select the desired font.
     c. Click OK.

3. Set the desired font size.
   - On the Home tab of the Ribbon, in the Font group, from the Font Size drop-down list, select the desired font size.
   - On the Mini toolbar, from the Font Size drop-down list, select the desired font size.
   - On the Mini toolbar, click the Grow Font or Shrink Font button to increase or decrease the font size by one point at a time.
   - Or, open the Font dialog box and select the desired font size in the Size list box.

4. Apply bold, italics, or underlining.
   - On the Ribbon, on the Home tab, in the Font group, click any combination of the Bold, Italic, or Underline buttons. To change the underline style, select a style from the Underline drop-down list.
   - In the Font dialog box, in the Font Style list box, select Regular, Italic, Bold, or Bold Italic, and select an underline style from the Underline Style drop-down list.
   - Or, on the Mini toolbar, select the desired options.

5. To apply font effects, in the Font dialog box, check the desired effects in the Effects section. Available effects include Strikethrough, Double Strikethrough, Superscript, Subscript, Shadow, Outline, Emboss, Engrave, Small Caps, All Caps, and Hidden.

6. Set the font case.
   a. On the Home tab, in the Font group, click the Change Case button to open the Change Case gallery.
   b. In the Change Case gallery, choose the desired font case. You can choose from Sentence Case, Lowercase, Uppercase, or Capitalize Each Word, or you can choose Toggle Case to reverse the current casing.

7. Set the font color.

- On the Home tab of the Ribbon, in the Font group, click the Font Color drop-down arrow, and select the desired color from the Font Color gallery.

- On the Mini toolbar, click the Font Color drop-down arrow, and select the desired color.

- Or, open the Font dialog box, click the Font Color drop-down arrow, select the desired color, and click OK.

Procedure Reference: Copy Formats with the Format Painter

To copy formats with the Format Painter:

1. Select the text that has the format you want to duplicate.

2. Click the Format Painter button in the Clipboard group on the Home tab or on the Mini toolbar. If you want to copy to multiple selections, double-click the Format Painter.

3. Select the text to which you want to copy the formatting. If you double-clicked the Format Painter button, it will remain active, and you can make additional selections to continue copying the format.

4. To deactivate the Format Painter, click it again or press Esc.

Repeat an Action versus Redo an Action

After you perform an action, such as typing text, you can quickly repeat the action by clicking the Repeat button on the Quick Access toolbar. To see what action you are going to repeat, point to the Repeat button; the name of the last action you performed is appended to the Repeat button's ScreenTip. You can also repeat actions by pressing F4 or Ctrl+Y.

Repeat is not the same as Redo. You can repeat any action, but the Redo command works only if you have first used the Undo command to undo a specific action.

ACTIVITY 3-1

Changing Font Appearance

Data Files:

Relocation Services.docx

Before You Begin

From the C:\084893Data\Formatting Text folder, open Relocation Services.docx.

Scenario:

You have created the company report that will be emailed to all your clients. However, while reviewing the document, you realize that some critical information might be lost amidst the pages of plain text. You will need to ensure that your clients don't miss this critical information even if they only give your document a quick glance.

What You Do	**How You Do It**
1. **Change the font of the text "Our Relocation Services" to Arial, 24 pt.**	a. At the beginning of the document, **select the text "Our Relocation Services".** b. On the Home tab, in the Font group, from the Font drop-down list, **select Arial.**

c. In the Font group, from the Font Size drop-down list, **select 24.**

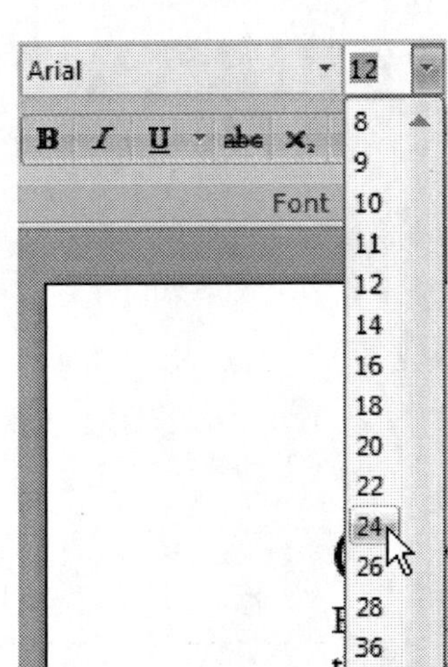

d. The text now appears as Arial, 24 pt. **Click after the word "Services"** to deselect the text.

2. **Change the font of the remaining titles to Arial, 24 pt.**

a. Below the fourth paragraph, **select the title "Our Relocation Staff".**

b. **Scroll down** to view the remaining titles.

c. In the seventh paragraph of the document, **hold Ctrl and select the title "Our Relocation Fees".**

Our·Relocation·Staff¶
Sales·Associates:·Dedicated·and·specially·trained·to·arrange·the·relocation·services·that·
our·clients·expect·and·deserve·within·specified·time·limits.¶
¶
Corporate·Division:·Presentations·on·the·area·and·on·Burke·Properties,·Inc.·Relocation·
services·for·all·size·corporations,·businesses,·and·companies.¶
¶
Our·Relocation·Fees¶
Our·fees·vary·depending·upon·the·scope·of·the·relocation.·We·can·help·relocate·one·
person·or·hundreds·of·people.·We·typically·require·5%-10%·down·at·signing.·However,·
we·are·always·willing·to·work·out·payment·options·that·meet·your·needs.¶

d. In the Font group, from the Font drop-down list, **select Arial.**

e. From the Font Size drop-down list, **select 24.**

f. **Click after the word "Staff"** to deselect the text.

<table>
<tr><td>3.</td><td>Change the casing of the report heading to uppercase.</td><td>a.</td><td>Select the heading "Our Relocation Services".</td></tr>
<tr><td></td><td></td><td>b.</td><td>In the Font group, click the Change Case button and choose UPPERCASE to convert all the letters in the title to uppercase.</td></tr>
</table>

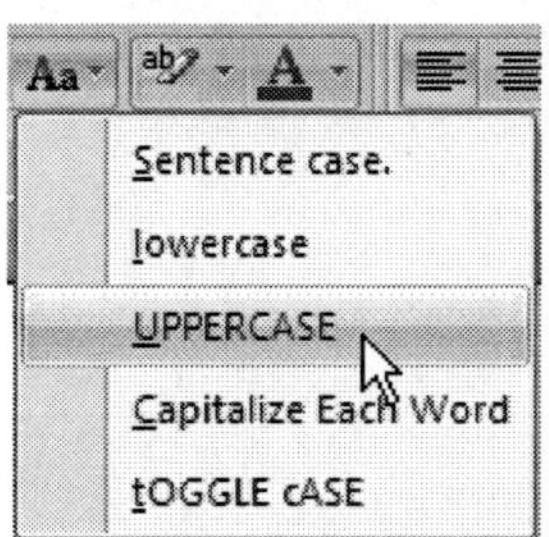

<table>
<tr><td>4.</td><td>Italicize the text, "Your Relocation Checklist".</td><td>a.</td><td>At the top of the document, in the first paragraph, select "Your Relocation Checklist".</td></tr>
<tr><td></td><td></td><td>b.</td><td>On the Mini toolbar, click the Italic button.</td></tr>
</table>

OUR·RELOCATION·SERVICES¶
Relocation·can·be·traumatic·for·everyone·involved.·We·offer·a·variety·of·publications·
that·can·help·ease·your·mind.·(We·strongly·recommend·*Your·Relocation·Checklist*.)·Also,·
the·dedicated·people·in·Burke·Properties·Relocation·Department·are·available·whenever·
you·need·them.·Here's·an·overview·of·what·we·offer.¶

<table>
<tr><td>5.</td><td>Repeat the italic font style on the text "unconditionally guarantee".</td><td>a.</td><td>In the last paragraph of the document, in the second line, select the text "unconditionally guarantee".</td></tr>
<tr><td></td><td></td><td>b.</td><td>On the Quick Access toolbar, click the Repeat button.</td></tr>
</table>

<table>
<tr><td>6.</td><td>Change the text color of the title to blue.</td><td>a.</td><td>Select the title "Our Relocation Services".</td></tr>
<tr><td></td><td></td><td>b.</td><td>In the Font group, click the Font Color drop-down arrow.</td></tr>
</table>

c. In the Font Color gallery, in the Standard Colors section, **select the eighth color** to apply a blue shade.

d. The text is now blue. **Click after the word "Services"** to deselect the text.

---

7. **Change the color of the text "money back" to green.**

a. In the last line of the document, **select the words "money back".**

b. In the Font group, **click the Font Color drop-down arrow.**

c. In the Font Color gallery, in the Standard Colors section, **select the sixth color** to apply a green shade.

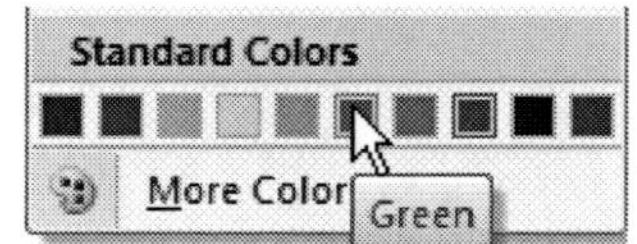

d. **Click after the word "back"** to deselect the text.

---

8. **Change the font of "Relocation Network:" to Arial, bold, 11 pt.**

a. In the second paragraph, **select "Relocation Network:"**

b. When you select the text, the Mini toolbar should appear. **Use the Mini toolbar to apply the Arial font, bold formatting, and 11 point size.**

c. **Click after the word "Network"** to deselect the text and hide the Mini toolbar.

---

9. **Apply the Double Underline and the Small Caps effect to the sub heading.**

a. **Select "Relocation Network".**

b. In the Font group, **click the Dialog Box Launcher button.**

c. The font settings that display in the dialog box match those of the selected text. From the Underline Style drop-down list, **select Double Underline.**

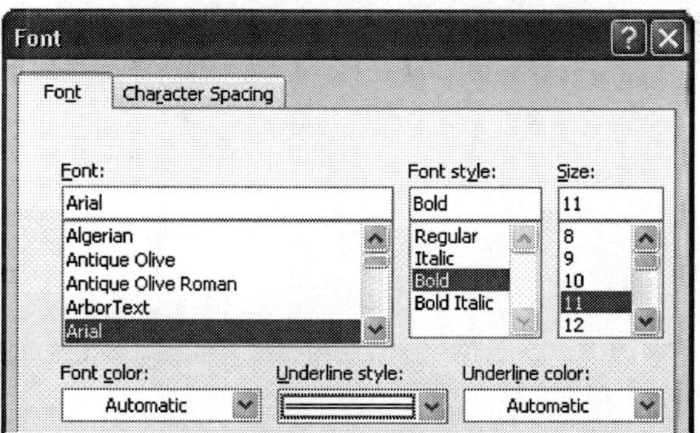

d. In the Effects section, **check the Small Caps check box.**

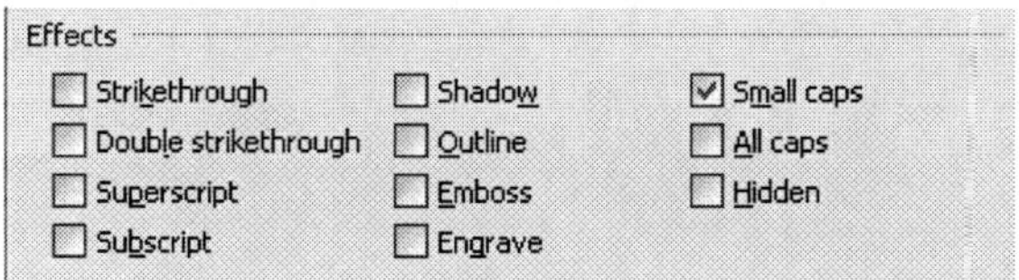

e. **Click OK** to apply the formatting.

---

10. Copy the text formatting of "Relocation Network" and apply it to "Relocation Package".

a. With the subheading selected, in the Clipboard group, **click the Format Painter button** to copy the existing text formatting.

b. The mouse pointer changes to an I-beam with a paint brush. In the third paragraph, **click and drag to select the subheading "Relocation Package:"** to apply the copied text formatting.

RELOCATION PACKAGE: Designed to be useful yet extensive enough to be serviceable. Included is information on area communities, schools, taxes, recreation, cultural activities, and many other materials about the area.¶

---

11. Apply the text formatting to the remaining four subheadings.

a. **Verify that "Relocation Package:" is still selected and, in the Clipboard group, double-click the Format Painter button.**

b. At the beginning of the fourth paragraph, **click and drag to select "Relocation Team:"** to apply the copied text formatting.

RELOCATION·TEAM: The·Relocation·Director,·Broker·and·Sales·Associates·create·a·total·sensitive·and·sensible·team·approach·while·meeting·the·unique·needs·of·every·person·or·family·being·relocated.¶

c. In the fifth, sixth, and eighth paragraphs, **click and drag to select "Sales Associates", "Corporate Division", and "Our Guarantee"** to apply the same formatting to all of them.

Our·Relocation·Staff¶
SALES·ASSOCIATES: Dedicated·and·specially·trained·to·arrange·the·relocation·services·that·our·clients·expect·and·deserve·within·specified·time·limits.¶
¶
CORPORATE·DIVISION:·Presentations·on·the·area·and·on·Burke·Properties,·Inc.·Relocation·services·for·all·size·corporations,·businesses,·and·companies.¶
¶
Our·Relocation·Fees¶
Our·fees·vary·depending·upon·the·scope·of·the·relocation.·We·can·help·relocate·one·person·or·hundreds·of·people.·We·typically·require·5%-10%·down·at·signing.·However,·we·are·always·willing·to·work·out·payment·options·that·meet·your·needs.¶
¶
OUR·GUARANTEE: We·are·so·sure·that·you·will·be·pleased·with·how·Burke·Properties·handles·your·real·estate·needs,·that·we·*unconditionally·guarantee*·your·complete·satisfaction·with·all·of·our·services·or·your·money·back…no·questions·asked!¶

d. In the Clipboard group, **click the Format Painter button** to turn off the tool.

e. **Save the document as *My Relocation Services.docx***

TOPIC B
Highlight Text

You have changed the appearance of selected text in a document by modifying font options. Another way to change text appearance, which does not involve changing the properties of the font, is to highlight the text. In this topic, you will highlight text.

Whether you highlight important lines in a book you're studying, or key points in a speech that you're attempting to memorize, you are merely ensuring that you do not miss any critical information. Word 2007 functions in the same way. By highlighting key words, phrases, or sentences in a document, you make it easier for the reader to locate important concepts or phrases by just glancing at the document.

Text Highlighting Options

Highlighting text draws attention to the important information in a document. The default text highlight color in a Word document is yellow. You can turn on the highlighter by clicking the Text Highlight Color button in the Font group. The mouse pointer then changes to an I-beam with a highlighter when you place it over text. You can then select the desired text to apply the default yellow highlight. If you want to modify the text highlight color, click the Text Highlight Color drop-down arrow and select the desired color. The selected color is displayed on the Text Highlight Color button. The highlighter remains active until you turn it off by clicking the Text Highlight Color button again.

Highlighter Tips

If you are going to print a document using a black and white printer, use a light color or gray to highlight text. This ensures that the text is still readable.

How to Highlight Text

Procedure Reference: Highlight Text in a Document

To highlight text in a document:

1. Select the text you want to highlight.
2. Apply a highlight color.
   - On the Home tab, in the Font group, click the Text Highlight Color button to apply the default color.
   - On the Home tab, in the Font group, click the Text Highlight Color drop-down arrow, and select the desired color from the Text Highlight Color gallery.
   - Or, display the Mini toolbar and select a highlight.
3. To remove highlighting, select the text and apply the No Color highlight.

ACTIVITY 3-2

Highlighting Text in a Document

Before You Begin

My Relocation Services.docx is open.

Scenario:

You want your manager to review the fee percentages in the company report that you created. You need to ensure that the fee percentage information stands out from the remaining text in the document. After you apply all the formatting, you need to evaluate the overall look and adjust the formatting, if necessary.

What You Do	**How You Do It**
1. **Highlight the text "money back" in yellow.**	a. In the last line of the document, **select the words "money back".**
	b. On the Home tab, in the Font group, **click the Text Highlight Color button.**
2. **Highlight the text "5%–10%" in red.**	a. In the previous paragraph, **select "5%–10%".**
	b. In the Font group, **click the Text Highlight Color drop-down arrow.**
	c. In the Text Highlight Color gallery, **select the Red shade** to highlight the text.
3. **Highlight an important phrase in yellow.**	a. In the last paragraph, **select the text, "we unconditionally guarantee your complete satisfaction"**
	b. In the Font group, **click the Text Highlight Color drop-down arrow.**
	c. In the Text Highlight Color gallery, **select Yellow (the first square in the first row).**
4. **Remove highlight from the text "5%–10%".**	a. In the seventh paragraph, **select "5%–10%".**
	b. In the Font group, **click the Text Highlight Color drop-down arrow.**

c. In the Text Highlight Color gallery, **select No Color** to remove the highlight.

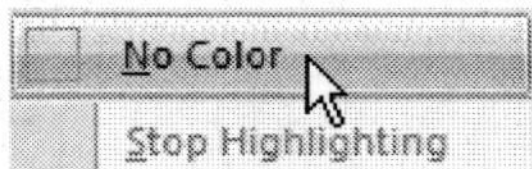

5. Update the saved document.

   a. **Click the Office button and choose Save.**

   b. **Close the document.**

Lesson 3 Follow-up

In this lesson, you formatted text by changing font appearance and by highlighting the text. Applying well-chosen text formatting to the relevant sections of a document can add visual interest and enhance your message while helping the reader understand the structure and layout of the information.

1. **How will you use text formatting to improve the appearance of your documents?**

2. **When do you think you would use highlighting as opposed to modifying font appearance?**

4 | Formatting Paragraphs

Lesson Time: 60 minutes

Lesson Objectives:

In this lesson, you will format paragraphs.

You will:

- Set tab stops to align text.
- Control paragraph layout.
- Add borders and shading to paragraphs.
- Apply a style to text.
- Create a bulleted and a numbered list.
- Manage text formatting.

Introduction

You applied character formatting to specific text. Now, you want to format paragraphs so the entire document is organized and easy to read. In this lesson, you will format paragraphs.

Consider two documents: one with paragraph formatting and one without. The one without the formatting is certainly legible, but the one with the formatting is much more attractive and easier for the reader to comprehend. By formatting the paragraphs in your documents, you can enhance their readability and visual appeal.

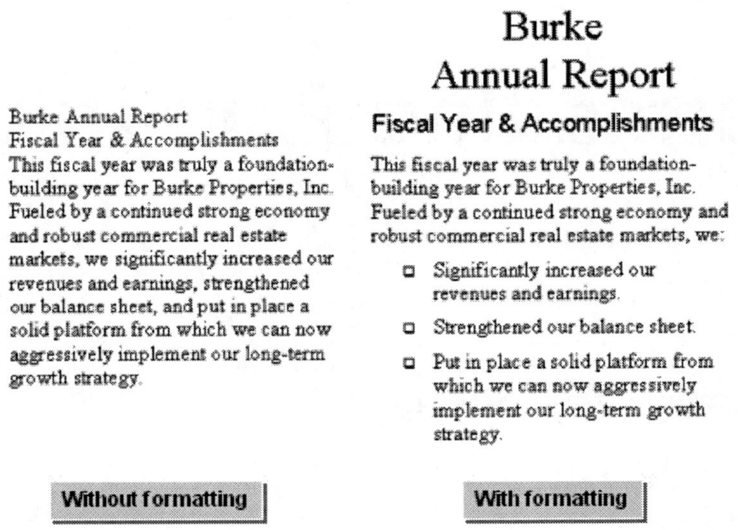

Figure 4-1: *A document without paragraph formatting (left), and one with paragraph formatting (right).*

TOPIC A

Set Tabs to Align Text

You have formatted text in a document by applying different fonts, styles, effects, and colors. Now, you need to arrange this text with appropriate spacing from the margins. In this topic, you will customize the default tab settings.

A tab stop is a very common paragraph alignment technique that is much easier to insert and manage electronically in Word than it is to insert manually in a paper document. You can use tabs as a simple way to align your text to give it a clean appearance as well as to organize related information visually on the page. You can use either default tab settings or custom tab settings in Word to ensure that your document is both professional looking and easy to read and understand.

Tabs

Definition:

Tabs or *tab stops* are document formatting options that enable you to align text to a specific horizontal location. You can set one or more tab stops within a paragraph of text. When you press the Tab key on the keyboard, the next text you type on that line will align with the next tab stop within the paragraph. By default, Word sets a left tab stop every half inch within every paragraph. You can use tabs to align text to the left, right, or center of the tab stop, or you can set other specialized tab types.

Paragraph formats such as tab settings are stored within the paragraph formatting mark. You can create a new paragraph with the same formatting by copying a paragraph mark.

Example:

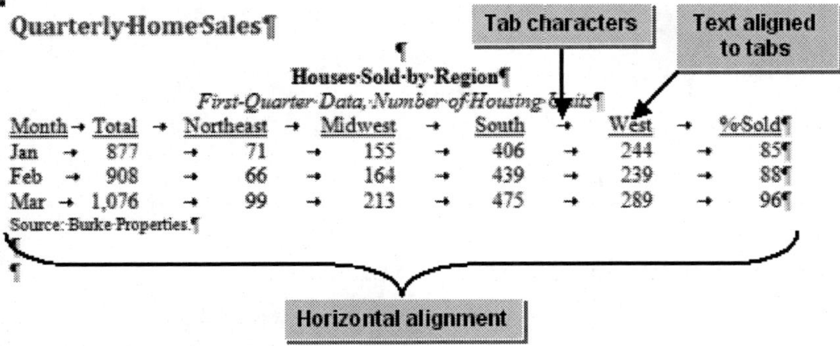

Figure 4-2: Text aligned using tabs.

The Word Rulers

Word provides you with two measuring tools, called *rulers,* to assist you in aligning documents. The rulers help you to identify and change tab settings and other document layout options, such as the page margins. By default, the unit of measurement for the ruler is inches. This can be changed to centimeters, millimeters, points, or picas, depending on your requirements. There are two rulers in Word: the horizontal ruler appears at the top and the vertical ruler appears at the extreme left of a document. The rulers are turned off by default; you can use the Show/Hide group on the View tab or the View Ruler button above the vertical scroll bar to display or hide the rulers.

Tab Stops on the Ruler

You can use the Tab Selector button above the vertical ruler to set five types of tab stops.

Tab Stop	*Description*
Left Tab stop	Sets the start of the text at the point of the tab stop and allows text to flow to the right of the tab stop.
Center Tab stop	Centers the text around the point of the tab stop.
Right Tab stop	Sets the end of the text at the point of the tab stop and allows text to flow to the left of the tab stop.
Decimal Tab stop	Allows text to align on the decimal point when numbers are used.
Bar Tab stop	Adds a vertical line through the paragraph at the tab position.

To display accurate measurements correct to 0.01 of an inch in the ruler, hold down Alt as you drag the tabs.

The Tabs Dialog Box

You can set and clear tab stops by using options in the Tabs dialog box.

Option	*Description*
Tab Stop Position	Displays all the tabs that have already been set.
Default Tab Stops	Specifies the spacing between default tab stops.
Alignment	Changes the tab stop selected in the Tab Stop Position text box to the type you specify.
Leader	Adds leader characters, which are dots, dashes, or lines that appear to fill the space before the tab stop.
Set	Sets the tab stop at the position specified in the Tab Stop Position text box.
Clear	Clears the tab stop at the position specified in the Tab Stop Position text box.

Option	Description
Clear All	Clears all the tab stops on the ruler.

How to Set Tab Stops

Procedure Reference: Set or Remove Tabs

To set or remove tabs:

1. Select the paragraph or paragraphs for which you need to set tab stops.

2. If you want to use the Ruler to set the tabs and the rulers do not appear, on top of the vertical scroll bar, click the View Ruler button.

3. Select the tab type.

   - Click the tab selector until the desired tab is displayed.

   - Or, in the Paragraph group on the Ribbon, click the Paragraph Dialog Box Launcher to open the Paragraph dialog box, click the Tabs button to open the Tabs dialog box, and select the desired tab type in the Alignment section.

4. Select the position to place the tab stops.

   - On the horizontal ruler, at the desired point, click to set the tab stop. To set more tabs of the same type, click additional locations.

   - Or, in the Tabs dialog box, in the Tab Stop Position text box, type the desired position for each tab and click Set. When you are done setting tabs, click OK.

5. To change the alignment of an existing tab, double-click the tab to open the Tabs dialog box. Select the desired tab stop position, and select a tab type in the Alignment section.

6. To add a leader, in the Tabs dialog box, in the Leader section, select the desired leader.

7. To move a tab stop, drag the tab to the new position on the ruler.

You cannot move an existing tab stop in the Tabs dialog box, but you can clear one stop and insert another at a new position.

8. To remove a tab stop, drag it off the ruler, or select it from the Tab Stop Position list in the Tabs dialog box and click Clear.

9. To clear all tabs for a paragraph, open the Tabs dialog box and click Clear All.

Line Breaks

A *line break* is a formatting mark used to end the current line before it wraps to the next line, but without starting a new paragraph. You can insert a line break by pressing Shift+Enter. The benefit of using a line break within a paragraph, rather than pressing Enter to start a new paragraph, is that the new line following the break remains part of the original paragraph and shares the paragraph's formatting.

ACTIVITY 4-1

Setting Tab Stops

Data Files:

Meeting Topics.docx

Before You Begin

From C:\084893Data\Formatting Paragraphs, open Meeting Topics.docx.

Scenario:

You have to submit a memo to all the regional managers of your company. As you are presenting the sales figures for each region, you need to make sure they are presented in a format that ensures easy readability.

What You Do	How You Do It
1. **Set a left tab stop** to indent text to the right.	a. Above the vertical scroll bar, **click the View Ruler button** to display the ruler.
	b. **Select the text "Attention:" through "Quarterly Sales Meeting", including the paragraph formatting mark.**
	c. On the left end of the horizontal ruler, above the vertical ruler, **verify that the Left Tab stop is displayed.**
	d. On the horizontal ruler, **click at 1.5 inches** to move the text after the tab to the 1.5 inch mark.

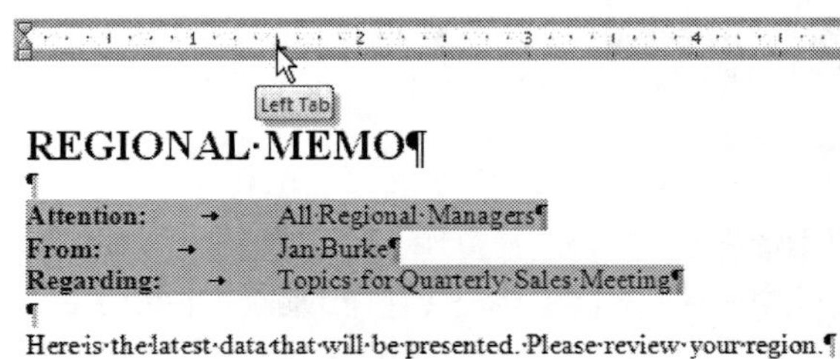

2. **Remove the center tab stop in the "Houses Sold by Region" data.**	a. Under the heading "First Quarter Data," **select the text "Month" through "96".**

b. On the horizontal ruler, **click and drag the center tab stop down and away from the horizontal ruler** to remove it and realign the text.

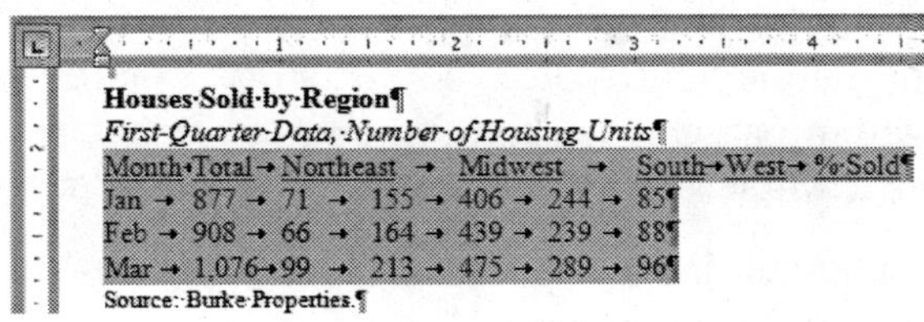

3. **Set right tab stops on the horizontal ruler.**

a. Above the vertical ruler, **click the tab selector two times** to display the Right Tab stop .

b. On the horizontal ruler, **click the mouse pointer at 1 inch.**

c. **Insert right tab stops at 2 inches, 3 inches, 4 inches, 5 inches, and 5.5 inches.**

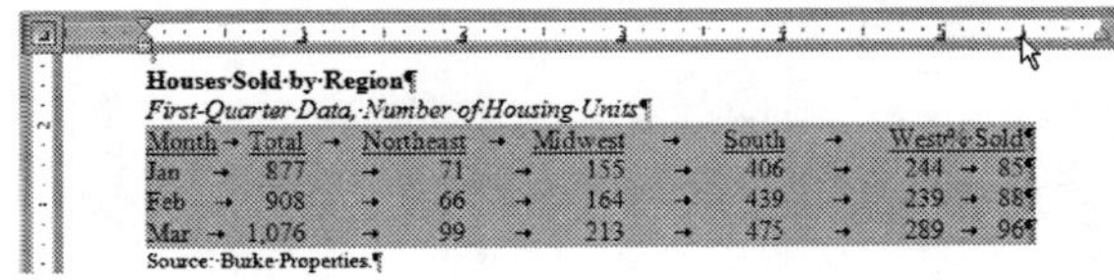

4. **Move the right tab stop from 5.5 inches to 6 inches.**

a. On the horizontal ruler, **select the tab stop at 5.5 inches and drag it to the 6 inch position.**

b. The text following the tab stop is realigned at 6 inches. **Save the document as *My Meeting Topics***

TOPIC B
Control Paragraph Layout

In the previous topic, you set tabs to control the placement of text on a line-by-line basis within paragraphs. You can also set paragraph formatting to control the layout of the paragraph as a whole. In this topic, you will control paragraph layout.

Paragraph layout options give you a great deal of control over the overall appearance of a paragraph on the page. By making the appropriate paragraph layout choices, you can configure common paragraph appearance settings such as paragraph alignment, paragraph margin settings, and spacing in and between paragraphs. With these layout options, you can add variety and a professionally published look to your Word documents.

Margins

Definition:

A *margin* is the blank area surrounding the text along the top, bottom, left, and right edges of a page. Margins determine the overall size of the document's text area in relation to the size of the paper it will print on, as well as the text's vertical or horizontal position on a page. They can also affect other layout options, which may be set in relation to the size of the margin.

Example:

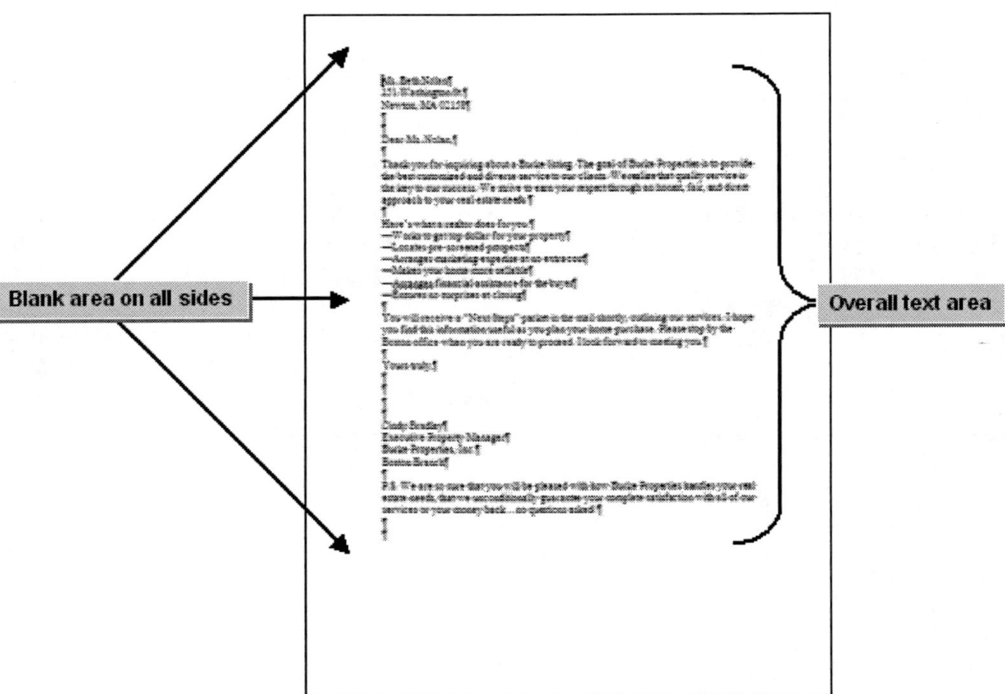

Figure 4-3: *Margins.*

Paragraph Alignment

The *paragraph alignment* setting determines how an entire paragraph is positioned horizontally between the left and right margins.

Option	Description
Align Text Left	The Align Text Left option aligns the left edge of the paragraph along the left margin. The paragraph's right edge appears ragged.
Center	The Center option aligns both sides of the paragraph equidistant from the left and right margins. Both the left and right edges of the paragraph appear ragged.
Align Text Right	The Align Text Right option aligns the right edge of the paragraph along the right margin. The paragraph's left edge appears ragged.
Justify	The Justify option aligns both sides of the paragraph evenly along the left and right margins. The paragraph's left and right edges are not ragged. Word adjusts the spacing between words so they stretch from the left margin to the right margin. When the last line of a justified paragraph is short, however, it won't be stretched.

Indents

Definition:

An *indent* enables you to align the left and right edges of a paragraph independently from the document margins. Indents affect only the paragraphs you have selected. Indents can be either positive, making the width of the paragraph narrower than the margin on one or both sides, or negative, making the width of the paragraph extend past the margin on one or both sides.

Another word for a negative indent is an outdent, because it makes the paragraph extend out into the margin space.

Example:

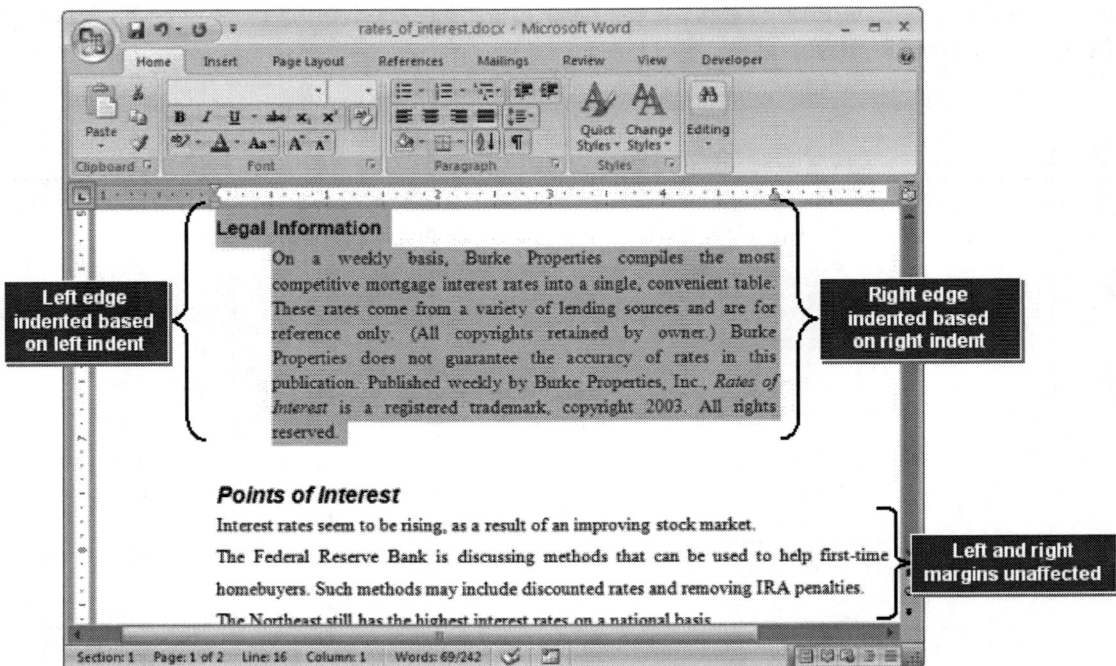

Figure 4-4: Indents in a Word document.

Using Indents for Quoted Material

A standard way to format a lengthy section of quoted material within a document is to place it within a paragraph that is indented on both sides.

Indent Markers

At the edges of the horizontal ruler of a Word document, there are four indent markers that you can drag to set the active paragraph's indentation.

Indent Marker	Description
First Line	Controls the left boundary for the first line of a paragraph.
Hanging	Controls the left boundary of every line in a paragraph, except the first line. This is generally used to align the first line with the margin and indent the remainder of the paragraph away from the margin.
Left	Controls the left boundary for every line in a paragraph.
Right	Controls the right boundary for every line in a paragraph.

Indentation Options

The indentation options in the Paragraph dialog box allow you to place indents on the ruler with an accuracy of 0.1 inch.

Option	Description
Left	Displays the current left indentation applied to the paragraph. You can either click the spin box to increase or decrease the indentation value, or just type the value in the Left text box.
Right	Displays the current right indentation applied to the paragraph. You can either click the spin box to increase or decrease the indentation value, or just type the value in the Right text box.
Special	Displays whether a First Line or Hanging indent marker has been set on the selected paragraph.
By	Displays the amount of indentation for any special indents in the selected paragraphs.
Mirror Indents	Enables you to set Inside and Outside margins for purposes of binding the document in a book or pamphlet format. The margins you set will be mirror images on facing pages of the document, because the inside edge of the paper is on the right for a left-hand page and the left for a right-hand page. For example, you can set a deeper Inside margin to provide more white space on the edge of the pages that will be inside the binding.

Text Spacing Options

Text spacing options in the Paragraph dialog box allow you to customize the amount of spacing between lines and paragraphs.

The spacing between paragraphs need not be uniform throughout a document.

Option	Description
Before	Adds the specified amount of space before the selected paragraph. The spacing before a paragraph can vary from 0 to 1584 points.
After	Adds the specified amount of space after the selected paragraph. The spacing after a paragraph can vary from 0 to 1584 points.
Line Spacing	Allows you to specify the amount of space between the lines in a paragraph. You can set single space, one and a half space, or double space, set the spacing to an exact or minimum amount, or choose Multiple to adjust the spacing by a percentage of the existing spacing.
At	Allows you to specify the amount of space between the lines in the selected text based on the option you have selected for Line Spacing.

Option	Description
Don't Add Space Between Paragraphs Of The Same Style	Adds no space between paragraphs that have the same style.

How to Control Paragraph Layout

Procedure Reference: Control Paragraph Layout

To control paragraph layout:

1. Select the paragraph or paragraphs you want to adjust.

2. Apply the desired paragraph alignment.

    - On the Home tab, in the Paragraph group, select the desired alignment: Align Text Left, Align Text Right, Center, or Justify.

    - Or, open the Paragraph dialog box, select the desired alignment from the Alignment drop-down list, and click OK.

If you want to change the alignment for only one paragraph, rather than selecting the paragraph, you can just place the insertion point in it.

3. Set the indent.

    - On the Home tab, in the Paragraph group, click the Increase Indent or Decrease Indent buttons to indent the left edge of the paragraph by 0.5 inches to the right or left. This limits your accuracy to a half an inch, and does not affect the first line, hanging, or right indents.

    - On the horizontal ruler, click and drag the appropriate indent markers to a new position. This is best suited for quick adjustments.

    - Or, open the Paragraph dialog box, change the Indentation settings, and click OK. This is the best way to get an accurate indentation setting because you can configure a value to an accuracy of 0.1 inch.

4. Set the spacing between lines in the paragraph.

    - Open the Paragraph dialog box and select a line spacing option. If you select At Least, Exactly, or Multiple, type the spacing value in the At spin box.

    - Or, click the Line Spacing drop-down list in the Paragraph group and select the desired amount of line spacing from the list of fixed spacing values. To set a custom value or different spacing options, click Line Spacing Options to open the Paragraph dialog box.

5. To set space before or after a paragraph, open the Paragraph dialog box and set the amount of space in the Before and After spin boxes.

ACTIVITY 4-2

Aligning Paragraphs

Before You Begin

My Meeting Topics.docx is open.

Scenario:

You decide to proof-read the memo you prepared before presenting it to the managers. During your review, you notice that the title of the memo does not appear at the center and the quarterly data is not easily distinguishable from the rest of the text. The disclaimer text blends in with the content of the memo, and the paragraphs are not spaced appropriately to enable your colleagues to take notes during the meeting. You decide to ensure that your document is easily readable and neatly presented.

What You Do	How You Do It
1. Align the title "Regional Memo" to the center of the document.	a. At the beginning of the document, **click before the title "Regional Memo."**
	b. On the Home tab, in the Paragraph group, **click the Center button** to center the title.

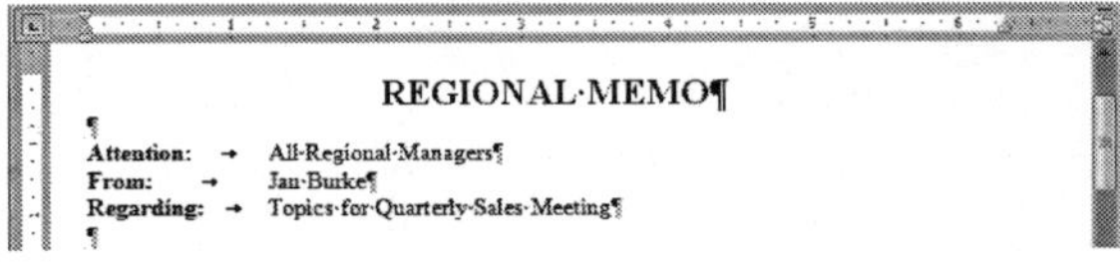

2. Center align the headings above the tabbed list.	a. **Select the text from "Houses Sold" through "Housing Units".**

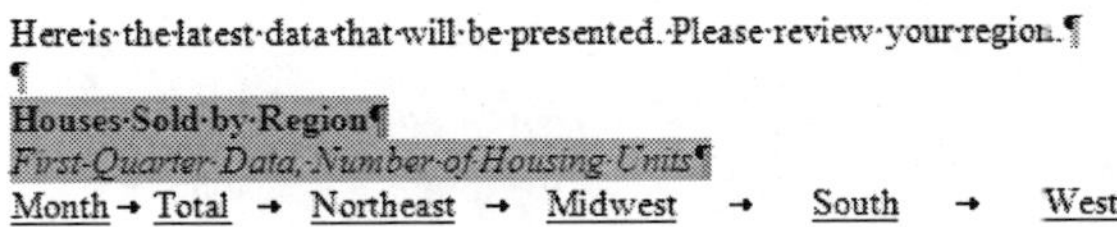

| | b. | In the Paragraph group, **click the Center button.** |

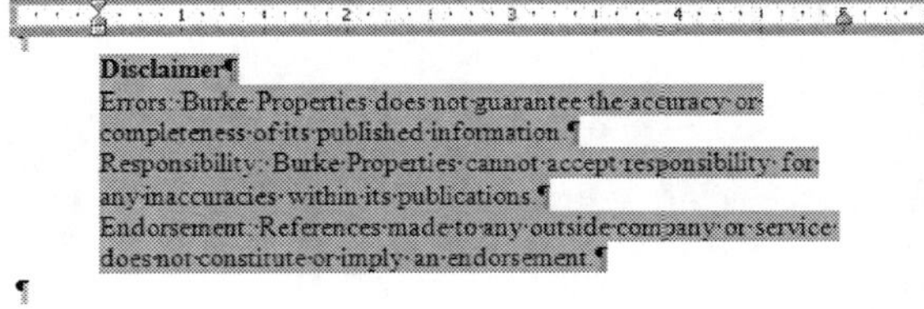

3.	**Set the right and left indents.**	a.	**Scroll down** to view the "Disclaimer" paragraph.
		b.	In the document, **select the "Disclaimer" heading along with the three paragraphs under it.**
		c.	In the Paragraph group, **click the Increase Indent button** to increase the indent by 0.5 inch.
		d.	On the horizontal ruler, **click and drag the Right Indent marker to the 5–inch mark.**

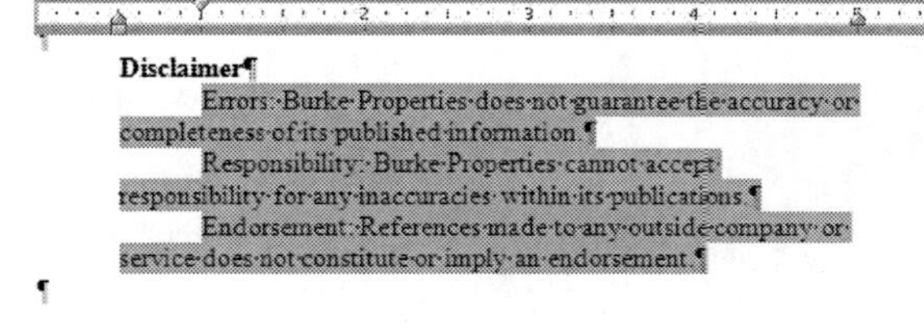

| 4. | **Indent the Disclaimer paragraphs by 0.25 inches.** | a. | At the end of the document, under the heading "Disclaimer", **select the text from "Errors" to "imply an endorsement." and the paragraph formatting mark after it.** |
| | | b. | On the horizontal ruler, **click and drag the First Line Indent marker two points to the right.** |

5. **Add 6 points of space before the title.**

a. **Scroll up the document and place the insertion point before the title "Houses Sold by Region".**

b. In the Paragraph group, **click the Dialog Box Launcher button.**

c. In the Paragraph dialog box, in the Spacing section, in the Before spin box, **click the up arrow** to change the spacing to 6 pt.

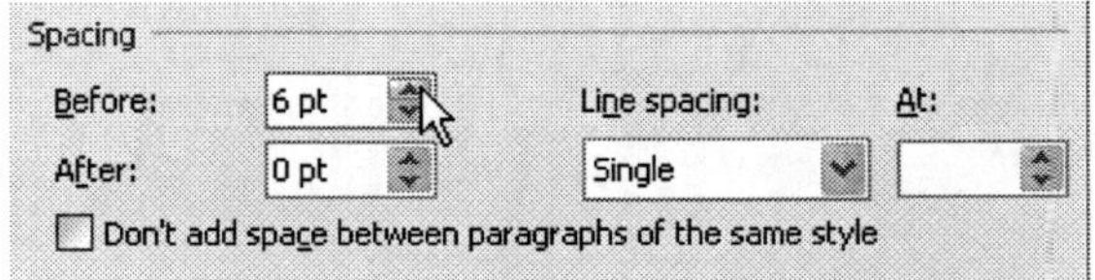

d. **Click OK** to apply the spacing and to close the dialog box.

6. **Add 6 points of space after the text "Source: Burke Properties."**

a. In the document, **place the insertion point before "Source: Burke Properties".**

b. In the Paragraph group, **click the Dialog Box Launcher button.**

c. In the Paragraph dialog box, in the Spacing section, in the After spin box, **click the up arrow** to change the spacing to 6 pt.

d. **Click OK** to apply spacing and to close the dialog box.

7. **Apply line spacing for the Action Items list.**

a. In the document, **select the heading "ACTION ITEMS" along with the three items below it.**

b. In the Paragraph group, from the Line Spacing drop-down list, **select 2.0** to increase the space between the list items.

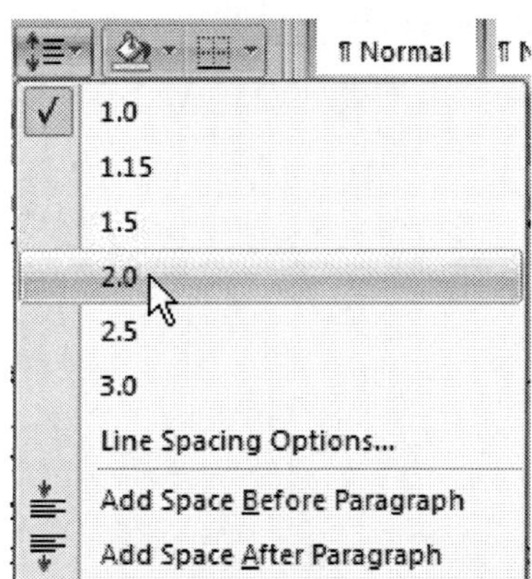

c. **Click in the text area** to deselect the text.

ACTION·ITEMS¶

●→ *Tim·will·distribute·the·data.*¶

●→ *Kris·will·print·the·inserts.*¶

●→ *Ryan·will·plan·the·next·meeting.*¶

d. **Save the document.**

TOPIC C
Add Borders and Shading

You have adjusted paragraph layout to improve readability. You now want to ensure that critical components of the text clearly stand out from the rest of the page. One way to do that is with border and shading options in Word. In this topic, you will add borders and shading to paragraphs.

Shaded paragraphs and borders draw attention to important content and help readers to locate critical ideas quickly. This ensures that readers who skim through documents do not miss out on any important information.

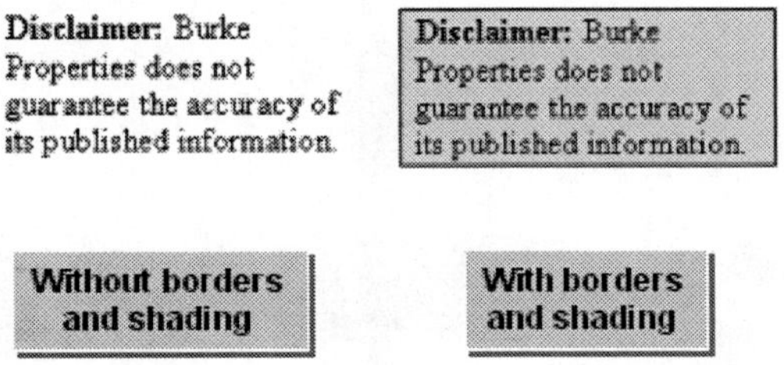

Figure 4-5: *A paragraph without borders and shading (left) and the same paragraph with borders and shading (right).*

Borders

Definition:

A *border* is a decorative line or pattern that is displayed around objects. The Border option in the Paragraph group of the Home tab allows you to apply the desired border to an object. There are different types of borders that can be applied to paragraphs, pages, and pictures to draw attention to the object to which they have been applied.

Custom art cannot be used for borders.

Example:

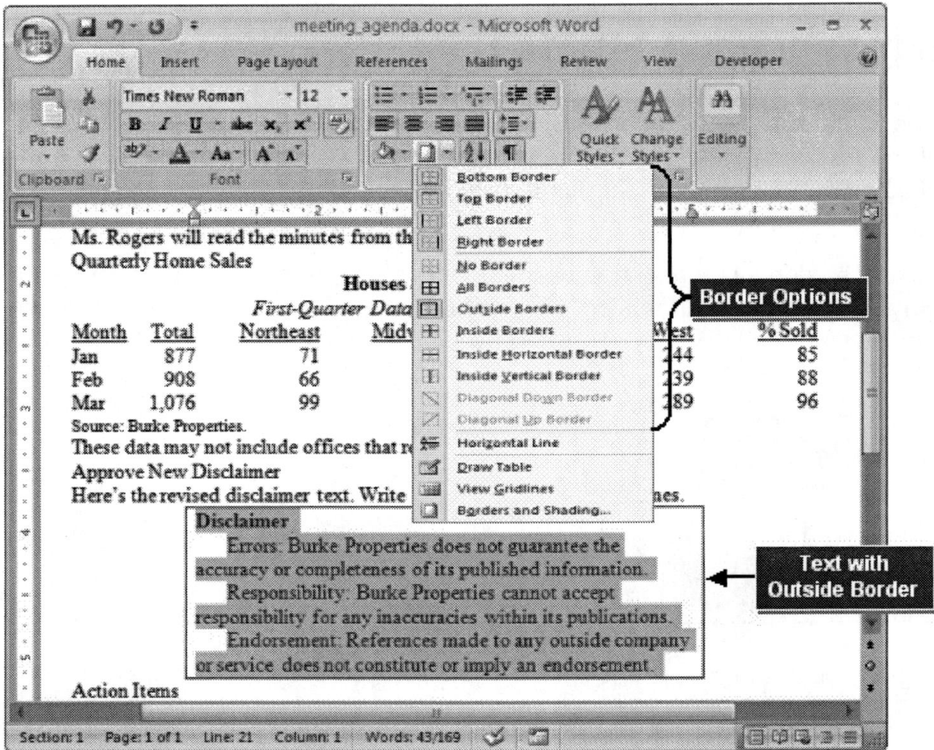

Figure 4-6: Border options in Word.

Border Types

Click the Border drop-down arrow in the Paragraph group of the Home tab to see a list of pre-defined border types.

Border Type	Description
Bottom Border	Inserts a line below the selected object or text.
Top Border	Inserts a line above the selected object or text.
Left Border	Inserts a line to the left of the selected object or text.
Right Border	Inserts a line to the right of the selected object or text.
No Border	Removes an already existing border on a selected object or text.
All Borders	Applies an outline to the selection and also inserts vertical and horizontal lines between items. This option works only for tables.
Outside Borders	Applies an outline to the selected object.
Inside Borders	Inserts vertical and horizontal lines between items. This option works only for tables.
Inside Horizontal Border	Inserts horizontal lines between the selected objects or text. This option works only for tables.
Inside Vertical Border	Inserts vertical lines between the selected objects or text. This option works only for tables.

Border Type	Description
Diagonal Down Border	Inserts a Descending Diagonal line. This option works only for tables.
Diagonal Up Border	Inserts an Ascending Diagonal line. This option works only for tables.

Additional Border Options

Apart from directly selecting a predefined border, there are also options in the Border drop-down list that allow users to customize and specify how the borders are displayed in a document.

Border Option	Description
Horizontal Line	Inserts a horizontal line on the line where the insertion point is placed.
Draw Table	Draws a table of the desired size.
View Gridlines	Shows or hides gridlines in tables.
Borders And Shading	Opens the Borders And Shading dialog box.

Shading

Definition:

Shading is a percentage of color that can be added to the background of objects. Shading can be used to highlight important information in a document or to apply a shadow effect. You can apply shading to a line, a paragraph, or table data. You can include an overall fill color, a pattern in a contrasting color, or both.

Example:

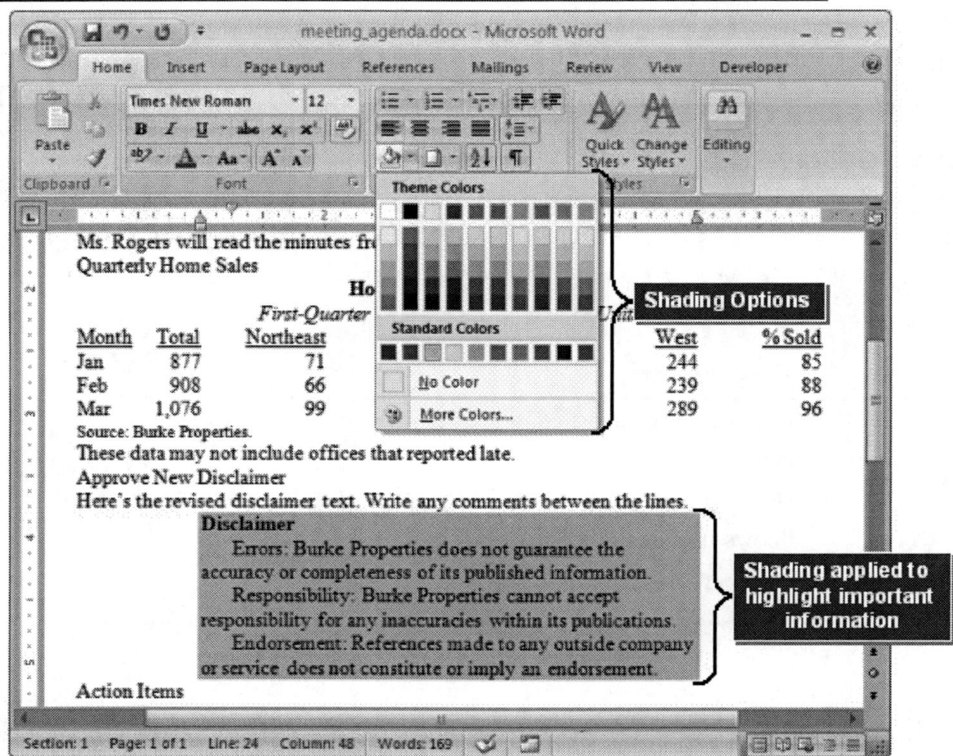

Figure 4-7: Shading in Word.

The Borders And Shading Dialog Box

The Borders And Shading dialog box has three tabs that allow you to specify the exact kind of border or coloring you would like to apply to the selected objects.

Tab	Contains Options To
Borders	Specify the type of border, its style, color, width, and the object to which it should be applied. It also shows a preview of the options that you set on the Borders tab.
Page Border	Specify the type of page border, its style, color, width, art, and object to which it should be applied. It also shows a preview of the options that you set on the Page Border tab.
Shading	Specify the fill color, the pattern and pattern color, and the object to which it should be applied in the document. It also shows a preview of the options that you set on the Shading tab.

Borders Options

The Borders tab in the Borders And Shading dialog box has a number of options that allow users to apply the desired border to objects in a document. These include the type of border you want to apply, the style, color, and width of the border line, custom border options, and a preview area where you can verify the appearance of your border selections. For example, you can select border types including box borders, shadow borders, and 3-D borders, and line styles such as single, double, or dashed, along with many other customizable border options.

How to Add Borders and Shading

Procedure Reference: Add a Border or Shading

To add a border or shading:

1. Select the paragraph or paragraphs to which you want to add a border or shading.

2. Apply the border.

    *   In the Paragraph group, click the Borders drop-down arrow and choose an existing border option to apply a predefined border.

    *   Or, from the Borders drop-down list, click Borders And Shading to open the Borders And Shading dialog box and select Custom Border Options. Click OK.

> The top and bottom borders extend from the Left Indent marker to the Right Indent marker.

3. Add the shading.

    a. Open the Borders And Shading dialog box and select the Shading tab.

    b. If you want to add an overall fill color, select the color from the Fill drop-down list.

    c. If you want to add a pattern, select the shading percentage or pattern from the Style drop-down list.

    d. If you selected a pattern, select a color for the pattern from the Color drop-down list.

    e. Click OK to apply the shading and close the dialog box.

4. To add a fill color only, click the Shading drop-down list in the Paragraph group and select the desired color.

5. To remove shading, select No Color for the fill and Clear for the pattern style.

ACTIVITY 4-3
Applying Borders and Shading to a Paragraph

Before You Begin:
My Meeting Topics.docx is open.

Scenario:
You have created a memo with the sales figures for all four quarters of last year. You need to make sure that all the regional managers of your company concentrate only on the data for the last quarter.

What You Do	**How You Do It**
1. **Apply a bottom border below the title.**	a. At the beginning of the document, **click before the title "Regional Memo."**
	b. On the Home tab, in the Paragraph group, **click the Borders drop-down arrow and choose Bottom Border.**

2. **Apply a box border for the "quarterly data" paragraph.**	a. In the document, **select the heading "Houses Sold by Region" along with the data below it and the text "Source: Burke Properties."**
	b. In the Paragraph group, **click the Borders drop-down arrow and choose Borders And Shading.**

c. In the Borders And Shading dialog box, in the Setting section, **select Box.**

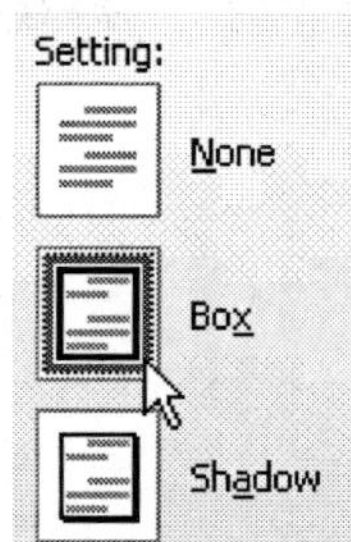

d. From the Width drop-down list, **select 1½ PT and verify that your selections appear in the Preview area.**

3. **Apply an orange shading to the "quarterly data" paragraph.**

a. In the Borders And Shading dialog box, **select the Shading tab.**

b. From the Fill drop-down list, in the Standard Colors section, **select Orange.**

c. **Click OK** to apply the borders and shading and close the dialog box.

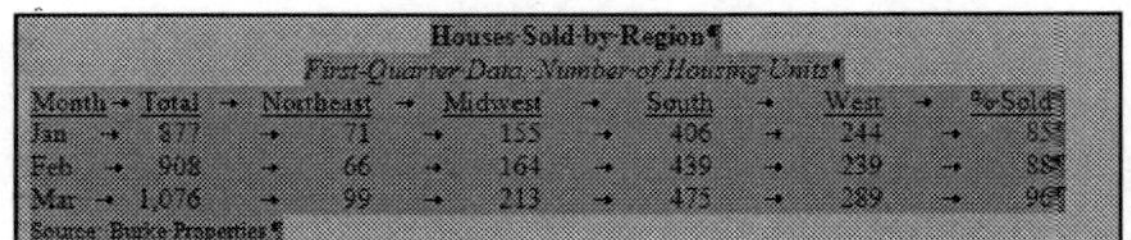

Houses Sold by Region¶					
First-Quarter Data. Number of Housing Units¶					
Month → Total →	Northeast →	Midwest →	South →	West →	% Sold¶
Jan → 877 →	71 →	155 →	406 →	244 →	85¶
Feb → 908 →	66 →	164 →	439 →	239 →	88¶
Mar → 1,076 →	99 →	213 →	475 →	289 →	96¶
Source: Burke Properties ¶					

d. **Click in the text area** to deselect the text.

4. **Apply the same border and shading options to different text.**

a. **Scroll down** to view the remaining text in the document.

b. In the document, **select the heading "Disclaimer" and the three paragraphs below it.**

c. On the Quick Access toolbar, **click the Repeat button** to repeat the shading.

> Disclaimer¶
>   Errors: Burke Properties does not guarantee the accuracy or completeness of its published information. ¶
>   Responsibility: Burke Properties cannot accept responsibility for any inaccuracies within its publications. ¶
>   Endorsement: References made to any outside company or service does not constitute or imply an endorsement. ¶

d. **Click anywhere in the text area** away from the text selection to deselect it.

e. **Save and close the document.**

TOPIC D
Apply Styles

You added borders and shading to paragraphs, in addition to making other formatting changes on selected text. Sometimes, you may want to reuse or apply several formatting options at the same time. In this topic, you will apply the default styles in Word 2007.

When creating official documents, you may want to apply specific design and typographical changes to them. Instead of accessing the options from across different dialog boxes, Word enables you to produce the desired output from preset style galleries. Styles help you quickly achieve consistent and customized design and formatting effects.

Word Styles

Definition:

A Word *style* is a named collection of appearance settings that can be applied to sections of a document as a group. Using a style can be quicker than applying individual formatting options, and it can ensure consistency of formatting throughout a document. A style may include text formatting options such as different typefaces, colors, and effects, as well as paragraph formatting options such as line spacing, borders, and shading. You can use built-in styles, modify existing styles, or create your own custom styles.

Example:

Figure 4-8: A document with various text styles applied.

Quick Styles in Word

Definition:

A *Quick Style set* is a package of styles that work well together that you can apply to a document as a group. By changing from one Quick Style set to another, you can apply design and formatting changes to a document all at the same time by switching from the styles in one set to their equivalents in another set. The styles in the current Quick Style set appear in the Styles group of the Home tab; you can scroll to select a style or click the More button to view the Quick Styles gallery. Word includes sever pre-defined Quick Style sets; you can build a new style or modify an existing style and then add it to the Styles gallery.

Example:

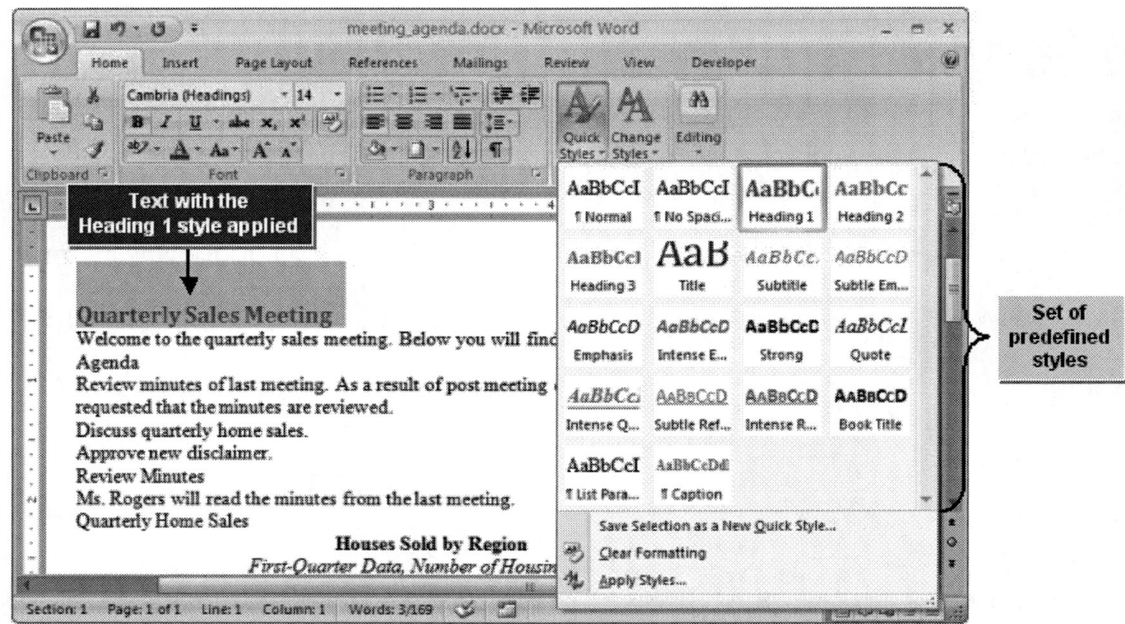

Figure 4-9: *Quick Styles in Word.*

The Styles Task Pane

The Styles task pane contains various options to work with styles.

When you open the Styles task pane, you might need to drag it to the edge of the window to dock it before you can see all of the options.

Option	Description
Clear All	Clears all the styles that have been applied to the selected text.
Styles	Displays the styles in the Styles gallery as a list.
Show Preview	Shows a preview of the styles.

Option	**Description**
Disable Linked Styles	Disables the styles that are linked.
New Style	Opens the Create New Style From Formatting dialog box where you can create a new style and add it to the styles list.
Style Inspector	Opens the Style Inspector dialog box where you can customize the formatting for a paragraph or the text you have selected.
Manage Styles	Opens the Manage Styles dialog box containing the tabs to edit, recommend, restrict, and set default styles.
Options	Opens the Styles Gallery Options dialog box where you can customize the Styles gallery.

The Apply Styles Task Pane

The Apply Styles task pane is used to modify or reapply a style that has already been applied to a document. On the Home tab, in the Styles group, click the More button and select Apply Styles to open the Apply Styles task pane. It can also be invoked by pressing Ctrl+Shift+S.

The Style Inspector

The Style Inspector task pane displays paragraph- and text-level formatting. It can be used to clear formatting at the paragraph—level or character—level. The Style Inspector can be displayed by clicking the Style Inspector button found within the Styles task pane.

How to Apply Styles

Procedure Reference: Apply a Style

To apply a style from the current Quick Style set:

1. Select the text to which you want to apply a style.
2. Apply the desired style to the selected text.
   - On the Home tab, in the Styles group, either scroll to select the style, or click the More button and select the desired style from the Styles gallery.
   - Or, on the Home tab, in the Styles group, click the Dialog Box Launcher button, and in the Styles task pane, select the desired style.

Changing the Quick Style Set

If you want to change to a different Quick Style set, click the Change Styles button in the Styles group, choose Style Set, and select the desired set. You can point to each style set name to see an instant preview of how text will look in that style set. When you choose a set, all the styles in your document will update to the equivalent styles in the new style set. For example, if you have applied the Heading 1 style in the default Quick Style set, when you change to a different set, the Heading 1 style in the new set will be applied to all the Heading 1 text in the document.

ACTIVITY 4-4

Applying Paragraph Styles

Data Files:

Meeting Agenda.docx

Before You Begin:

From the C:\084893Data\Formatting Paragraphs folder, open Meeting Agenda.docx.

Scenario:

You have been asked to make a presentation to some of your new clients. The presentation handouts contain information such as Houses Sold by Region, as well as the Disclaimer of the company. Your manager has approved the content in these handouts and asked you to ensure that the title and headings are distinct. You decided not to apply borders or shading.

What You Do	**How You Do It**
1. **Apply the Heading 1 style to "Quarterly Sales Meeting."**	a. At the beginning of the document, **click before the title "Quarterly Sales Meeting."**
	b. On the Home tab, in the Styles group, **click the More button** ⯆ **and select Heading 1.**
	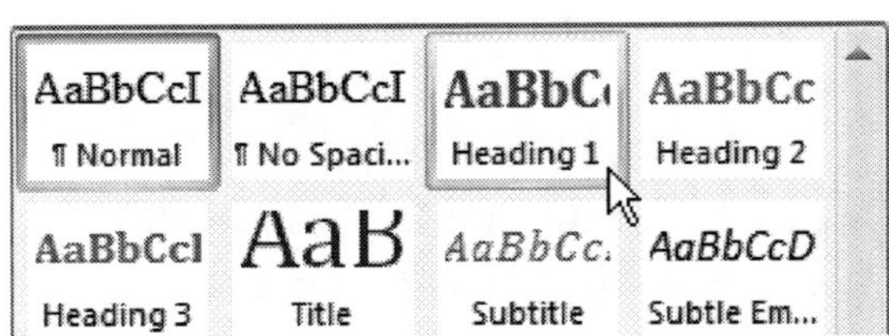
2. **Apply the Heading 2 style to "Agenda".**	a. In the third line of the document, **place the insertion point at the beginning of the heading "Agenda".**
	b. In the Styles group, **click the More button and select Heading 2.**

3. **Apply the Subtle Reference style to the heading "Review Minutes".**

a. In the ninth line of the document, **select "Review Minutes".**

b. In the Styles group, **click the More button.**

c. In the fourth row, second column, **select the Subtle Reference style.**

d. In the document, **select the headings "Quarterly Home Sales", "Approve New Disclaimer", and "Action Items".**

e. In the Styles group, **click the More button and select the Subtle Reference style.**

f. **Save the document as** *My Meeting Agenda*

TOPIC E
Create Lists

You applied in-built styles to specific paragraphs in your document. While reviewing some of these formatted paragraphs, you decide that the content in some of them will be better presented if displayed in a sequential order. In this topic, you will create bulleted and numbered lists.

Lists of various types can greatly improve the clarity and readability of text that groups similar items together or provides a series of steps. Instructions presented in a list can be much easier to follow that instructions presented in a continuous paragraph. Presenting information in a list not only enhances how it looks, but also increases readability. By using the list options in Word, you can create much more dynamic and effective documentation.

Driving Directions to Burke from the North
Take Interstate 93 SOUTH to the Callahan Tunnel exit. At the end of the off ramp, go straight through the intersection, following signs for "Waterfront Surface Artery." At the second light, turn right on South Ave. Burke Properties is ahead, about three blocks on the left.

Instructions in a paragraph

Driving Directions to Burke from the North
1. Take Interstate 93 SOUTH to the Callahan Tunnel exit.
2. At the end of the off ramp, go straight through the intersection, following signs for "Waterfront Surface Artery."
3. At the second light, turn right on South Ave. Burke Properties is ahead, about three blocks on the left.

Instructions in a numbered list

Figure 4-10: *Instructions in a paragraph without a list (left). Instructions in a list (right).*

Lists

Definition:

A *list* is a data grouping method in which the items in the group are displayed one after the other. A list often has lead-in text that provides a brief description about the items following it. There can be any number of items in a list. Word allows you to create single- or multi-level lists that use various styles of numbers or bullets.

Example:

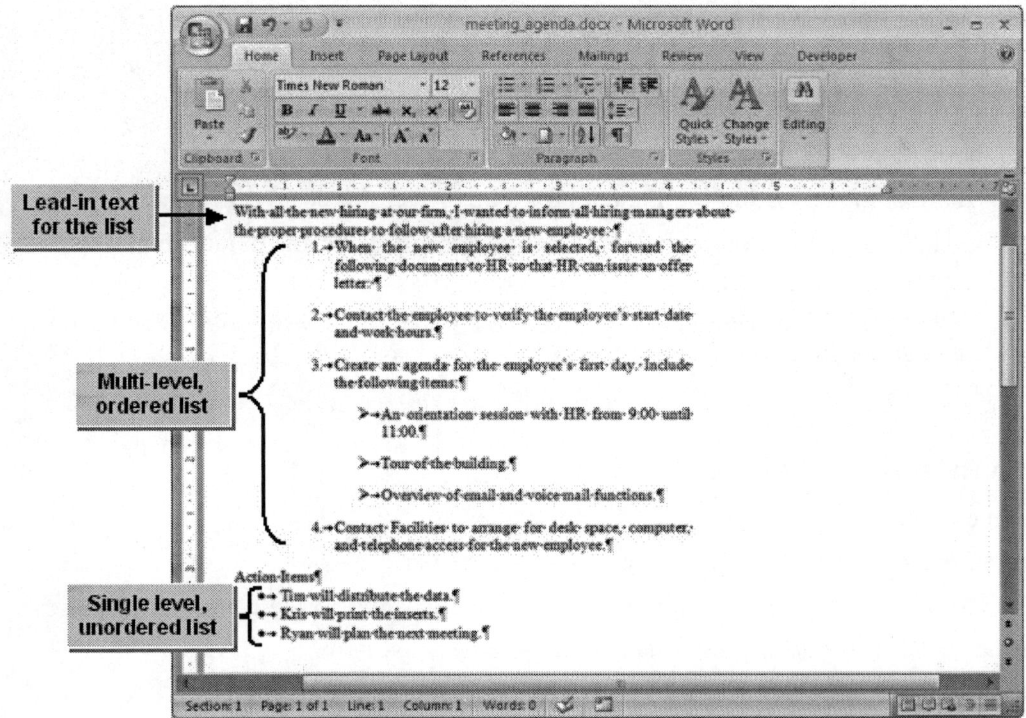

Figure 4-11: Single-level and multi-level lists.

Bulleted and Numbered Lists

There are two main types of lists in Word.

List Type	Description
Numbered (Ordered)	A *numbered list,* also called an *ordered list,* is a list that is used to denote a ranking among items or a sequence that must be followed. You can customize the list by choosing different alphabetic or number formats, such as numeric or Roman. Numbered lists can be multi-level and the items in a list may be a single word, a short phrase, or a paragraph.
Bulleted (Unordered)	A *bulleted list,* also called an *unordered list,* is a list that is used to denote a group of equally significant items. They are grouped under the same heading. You can customize the list by choosing different bullet styles. Bulleted lists can be multi-level. Each bulleted item in a list may be a single word, a short phrase, or a paragraph.

How to Create Lists

Procedure Reference: Create a List from Existing Text

To create a list from existing text:

1. Select the paragraph(s) that will be transformed to a list.
2. Create the list.
   - On the Home tab, within the Paragraph group, select the desired list type.
     - Click the Bullets button to create a bulleted list using the default bullet list settings.
     - Click the Numbering button to create a numbered list using the default numbered list settings.
   - Or, right-click the selected paragraph and select the list style.

Procedure Reference: Create a New List

To create a new list:

1. Place the insertion point where you want to start the list.
2. On the Home tab, in the Paragraph group, select the desired list style.
3. Type the first list item and press Enter to add the next list item.
4. If necessary, add more items to the list.
5. To end the list, press Enter twice, or click the appropriate list button again.

Procedure Reference: Remove Bullets and Numbering

To remove bullets and numbering:

1. Select the desired list.
2. Click the appropriate button in the Paragraph group.
   - Click the Bullets button to remove bullets.
   - Click the Numbering button to remove numbering.

Customizing List Formats

You can create a customized list or change the format of a list by selecting the list and right-clicking the selected area. From the menu, choose either Bullets, to see bullet formats, or Numbering, to see the various numbering formats. Click Define New to set custom list formatting.

AutoFormat Lists As You Type

When you want to start a new list, you can use the AutoFormat As You Type option in Word. To start a bulleted list, type an asterisk (*), press Tab, type the list item, and press Enter. Word will convert the asterisk into a bullet and begin a bulleted list for you. To start a numbered list, type the first number of the list and any trailing punctuation such as a period or open parenthesis. Press Tab, type the list item, and press Enter. Again, Word will begin the numbered list using the numbering format you want. You can use the AutoCorrect dialog box to control automatic list settings.

ACTIVITY 4-5

Creating Numbered and Bulleted Lists

Before You Begin
My Meeting Agenda.docx is open.

Scenario:
You need to prepare the agenda for a meeting and circulate it among your colleagues. In the agenda, you need to list out details that will be covered during the meeting. You also decide to include the action items.

What You Do	How You Do It
1. **Format paragraphs as a numbered list.**	a. Below the heading "Agenda," **select the three paragraphs of text.**
	b. On the Home tab, in the Paragraph group, **click the Numbering button** to convert the text to a numbered list.
	Agenda¶ 1.→ Review minutes of last meeting. As a result of post meeting discussions, it has been requested that the minutes are reviewed.¶ 2.→ Discuss quarterly home sales.¶ 3.→ Approve new disclaimer.¶
2. **Add a fourth item to the list.**	a. At the end of the numbered list, **place the insertion point after "Approve new disclaimer".**
	b. **Press Enter** to start a new list item.
	c. **Type *Assign action items***

3. **Create a bulleted list.**

   a. **Scroll to the bottom of the document, and place the insertion point at the end of the document in the blank line.**

   b. In the Paragraph group, **click the Bullets button** to create a new empty bullet point.

   c. In the new bullet point, **Type *Tim will distribute the data.***

   d. **Press Enter** to create a second bullet point.

   e. **Type *Kris will print the inserts.***

   f. **Press Enter** to include a new bullet point.

   g. **Type *Ryan will plan the next meeting.***

   h. **Press Enter** to include a new bullet point.

   i. **Press Enter** to end the bulleted list.

   j. **Save the document and close it.**

TOPIC F
Manage Formatting

In the previous topics, you applied various types of paragraph formatting. Once you have completed all your formatting, you might need to manage the formatting by copying, deleting, or replacing it. In this topic, you will manage formatting.

Once the formatting that you choose to apply to your documents becomes more complex than the simple addition of bold fonts or italics, you might find that you need to manage the formatting by locating where specific formatting was used, applying a set of formats from one section of text to another, or removing specific formats from a section of text. Tasks like this can be inefficient to accomplish by visually scanning a document and manually copying or removing formatting. Microsoft Word provides a set of tools that you can use to manage complex document formatting with efficiency and ease.

The Reveal Formatting Task Pane

The Reveal Formatting task pane can help with many format management tasks. The options in the Reveal Formatting task pane help you to identify specific formatting options that have been applied to a text selection, including font, alignment, indents, document margins, and layout. The Reveal Formatting task pane lets you compare the formatting of one section to that of another, select text with similar formatting, and apply or clear formats.

Clear Formatting Options

Sometimes, instead of changing the formatting on an item, you may wish to remove all the existing formatting and reset the selection's appearance to the default. If you need to clear the formatting in a selection, you can use the Reveal Formatting task pane, the Styles task pane, the Style Inspector dialog box, or the Clear Formatting button in the Font group on the Ribbon.

Find and Replace Text Formatting Options

In some cases, you might want to find all instances where you have applied a particular format, or you might want to replace one set of format options with another. You can use the Format drop-down menu in the Find And Replace dialog box to search for a specific format option and replace it with a desired format. You can search for and replace font and paragraph formatting, tabs and tab settings, styles, highlighting, and other formatting options.

How to Manage Text Formatting

Procedure Reference: Manage Text Formatting with the Reveal Formatting Task Pane

To manage text formatting with the Reveal Formatting task pane:

1. On the Home tab, in the Styles group, click the Dialog Box Launcher button to display the Styles task pane.

2. If the Styles task pane is not docked, you might not see the Style Inspector button. Drag the Styles task pane to the edge of the Word window to dock it.

3. In the Styles task pane, click the Style Inspector button.

4. In the Style Inspector task pane, click the Reveal Formatting button to display the Reveal Formatting task pane.

5. To show more of the document window, close the Styles and Style Inspector task panes.

6. To reveal text formatting, select the desired text in the document. The Reveal Formatting pane will display the details of both Font and Paragraph formatting.

 You can also see the Font, Font Styles, and Font Size of the selected text in the Fonts group of the Home tab.

7. Perform the desired format management task.

   - To clear font and paragraph formatting from a selection, move the mouse pointer over the Selected Text box, click the drop-down arrow and choose Clear Formatting.

   - To make the format of a selection match the format of the text around it, click the Selected Text drop-down arrow and choose Apply Formatting Of Surrounding Text.

   - To select text with similar formatting, click the Selected Text drop-down arrow, and choose Select All Text With Similar Formatting. You can then clear the formatting or apply the surrounding formatting to all the selections as a group.

   - To compare the formatting of two selections, check the Compare To Another Selection check box and then select the second portion of text in the document. The Reveal Formatting pane will list the formatting differences.

8. Close the Reveal Formatting task pane.

Procedure Reference: Clear Text Formatting

To clear text formatting:

1. Select the text that contains the formatting you want to reset.

2. Clear all formatting.

   - Open the Styles task pane and select Clear All.

   - Or, open the Style Inspector dialog box and select Clear All.

3. To clear selected formatting, open the Style Inspector dialog box and click the Clear Paragraph Formatting or Clear Character Formatting buttons.

Procedure Reference: Find and Replace Text Formatting

To find and replace text formatting in your document:

1. Click at the beginning of the document.

2. On the Home tab, in the Editing group, click the Replace button.

3. In the Find And Replace dialog box, in the Find What text box, delete any unwanted text and formatting options.

4. Set the Find Font options.

   a. Click the More button.

   b. In the Replace section, click Format and select Font.

   c. In the Find Font dialog box, select the desired font attributes you want to find.

   d. Click OK.

5. In the Replace With text box, delete unwanted text and formatting options.

6. Set the Replace Font options.

   a. Click the More button to show the Replace options.

   b. Click Format and from the drop-down list, select Font.

   c. In the Replace Font dialog box, select the desired font attributes you want to use instead of the existing format.

   d. Click OK.

7. Replace instances, as needed.

8. In the Microsoft Office Word message box, click OK.

9. Close the Find And Replace dialog box.

If you change your mind about a replace operation, click the Undo button on the Quick Access toolbar. If you use the Replace button, Word will undo the replacements one by one. If you used the Replace All button, Word will undo all of the replacements at the same time.

Removing Formats from a Prior Search

When you display the Replace tab in the Find And Replace dialog box, some font formats may already be displayed in the Find What and Replace With text boxes, perhaps left over from a previous task. Before you begin a new search, you should remove the formats so that they don't interfere with your new search. To remove the formats from the Find or Replace tabs of the Find and Replace dialog box, click More to display the Search and Replace options, and click the No Formatting button to remove the formats.

ACTIVITY 4-6

Clearing Text Formatting

Data Files:

Relocation Services.docx

Before You Begin:

From the C:\084893Data\Formatting Paragraphs folder, open Relocation Services.docx.

Scenario:

You have to submit a business report to the clients of your company. While reviewing the document, you find that because you are distracted by too many formatting inconsistencies, you are unable to focus on all the ideas stated within the document. You will remove some formatting to focus your readers' attention back to the content.

What You Do	**How You Do It**
1. **Determine the existing formatting for the "unconditionally guarantee" text.**	a. **Press Ctrl+End** to navigate to the end of the document.
	b. In the last paragraph of the document, **select the text "unconditionally guarantee".**
	c. On the Home tab, in the Styles group, **click the Dialog Box Launcher button.**
	d. In the Styles task pane, **click the Style Inspector button.**
	e. In the Style Inspector task pane, **click the Reveal Formatting button** to display the Reveal Formatting task pane.
	f. The font attributes include the Times New Roman font, 12 pt, Italic. The character option is Highlight. **Close the Style Inspector task pane.**
	g. **Close the Styles task pane.**

2. **Clear the Italic font attribute from the "unconditionally guarantee" text.**

   a. In the Reveal Formatting task pane, **move your mouse pointer over the Selected Text text box** to reveal the drop-down arrow.

   b. **Click the Selected Text drop-down list and select Clear Formatting** to clear the Italic font attribute but not the highlight.

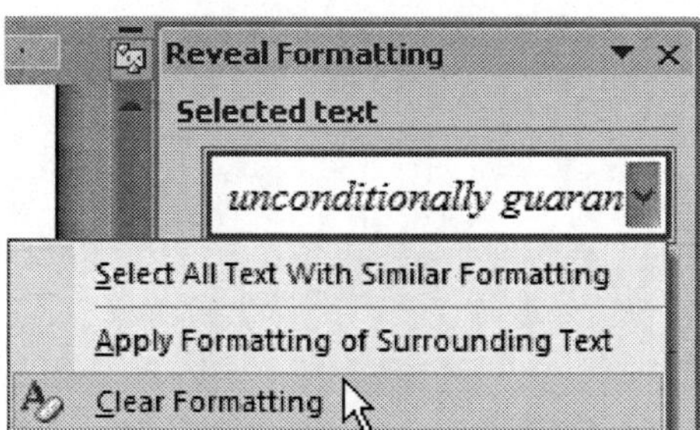

   c. **Verify that the italics have been removed, but not the highlight.**

3. **Clear the green font color of the text "money back".**

   a. In the last line of the document, **select "money back."**

   b. In the Reveal Formatting task pane, in the Formatting Of Selected Text list, **verify that the Font Color of the selected text is Green.**

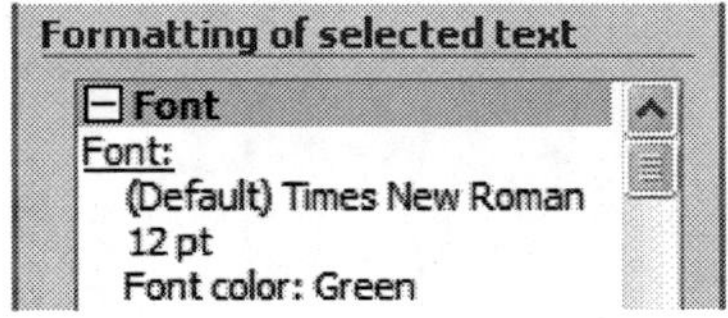

   c. In the Reveal Formatting task pane, **move your mouse pointer over the Selected Text text box** to reveal the drop-down arrow.

   d. **Click the Selected Text drop-down list box and select Clear Formatting.**

e. In the Reveal Formatting task pane, **verify that the Font Color attribute has been successfully removed.**

f. **Click after the word "back"** to deselect the selection.

g. **Close the Reveal Formatting task pane.**

h. **Save the file as *My Relocation Services.docx***

ACTIVITY 4-7

Finding and Replacing Text Formatting

Before You Begin:

My Relocation Services.docx is open.

Scenario:

Your company report is ready for your manager to review. You decide to proof-read the document one last time and notice that a few titles are formatted in Arial, while others are in a different style. To maintain consistency, set Tahoma as the font for all the occurrences of Arial.

What You Do	How You Do It
1. Set Arial as the font to search for.	a. **Place the insertion point at the beginning of the document.**
	b. On the Home tab, in the Editing group, **click Replace.**
	c. In the Find And Replace dialog box, **click More.**
	d. In the Replace section, **click Format.**
	e. From the Format drop-down list, **select Font.**
	f. In the Find Font dialog box, in the Font list box, **scroll down, select Arial and click OK.**
2. Set Tahoma as the replacement font.	a. In the Find And Replace dialog box, **click in the Replace With text box.**
	b. In the Find And Replace dialog box, in the Replace section, **click Format and choose Font.**
	c. In the Replace Font dialog box, in the Font text box, **type *Tahoma* and click OK.**

d. **Delete any text in the Find What And Replace With text boxes.**

e. **Click Less to close the advanced options.**

3. **Replace all instances of Arial with Tahoma.**

   a. In the Find And Replace dialog box, **click Replace All.**

   b. In the Microsoft Office Word message box, **click OK.**

4. **Clear the font formats in the Find And Replace dialog box.**

   a. In the Find And Replace dialog box, **verify that the cursor is in the Find What text box.**

   b. **Click More** to display the advanced Find options.

   c. In the Replace section, **click No Formatting.**

   d. **Click in the Replace With text box.**

   e. In the Replace section, **click No Formatting.**

   f. **Click Close.**

   g. **Save and close the document.**

Lesson 4 Follow-up

In this lesson, you made a document easier to read and understand by applying paragraph formatting techniques. You also took advantage of Word's ability to apply several formats simultaneously.

1. **What text formatting will you use to enhance the text in your documents? Why?**

2. **When formatting your documents, what Word tools will be most advantageous to you and why?**

5 | Adding Tables

Lesson Time: 60 minutes

Lesson Objectives:

In this lesson, you will add tables to a document.

You will:

- Create a table.
- Modify the table structure.
- Format a table.
- Convert text to a table or tables to text.

Introduction

Up to this point in the course, you have entered and modified text primarily in paragraph form in a document. In addition to text that is structured into paragraphs, Word enables you to include text that is structured in the form of a table. In this lesson, you will add tables to your documents to organize and enhance information.

Sometimes, when data is presented as a list or a paragraph, it can be difficult for readers to understand the content. When you use tables appropriately, they can significantly improve reader comprehension by enabling you to organize your information and eliminate unnecessary words.

TOPIC A

Create a Table

In this lesson, you will add tables to documents. The first step in adding a professional-looking table is to create the basic table and its data. In this topic, you will create tables to represent data.

Presenting textual information is what word processing is all about. But, when that text contains statistical or numerical data, the data often gets buried, making it difficult to read. Usually, the reader will benefit from seeing the data arranged in columns and rows. Tables make information more readily accessible to the reader with the least amount of effort by you.

Tables

Definition:

A *table* is a grid-style container used to organize text, data, or pictures. Tables consist of boxes called cells that are arranged in vertical columns and horizontal rows. A table can have specialized table formats such as borders drawn around some or all of the cells. The default is a thin black border around every cell.

Example:

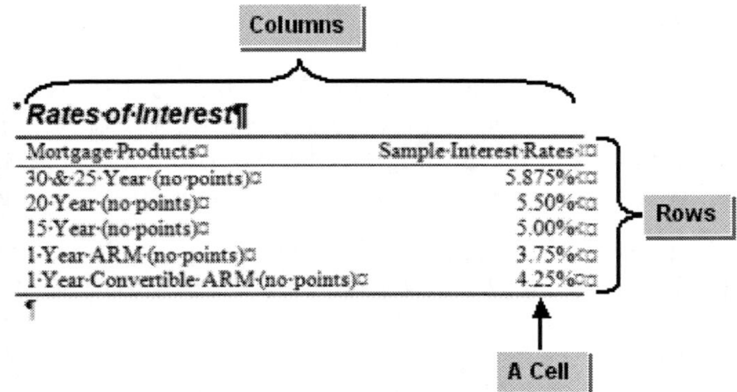

Figure 5-1: *A table with data entered into it.*

Non-printing Characters in Tables

There are several non-printing characters that are specific to tables. Each cell contains an end-of-cell marker to indicate the end of each cell. To the right of each row is an end-of-row marker that indicates the end of the row. A column marker appears in the ruler at the boundary of each column. You can use these markers to select table elements. In addition to these markers, Word also displays non-printing gridlines around the table cells. If a table has borders applied to it, gridlines are beneath the borders.

Gridlines are sometimes called boundaries. On the Table Tools Layout contextual tab, in the Table group, click View Gridlines to show or hide gridlines on the screen.

Table Creation Options

To create a table, you can select an option from the Table drop-down list on the Insert tab.

Option	Description
Table grids	Allows you to move the mouse pointer over the grids and click to insert a table with the desired number of rows and columns. This option automatically defines the column delimiters.
Insert Table	Displays the Insert Table dialog box with options to create a table.
Draw Table	Enables you to manually draw a table.

Table Navigation Methods

Although you can click to select table cells to enter text, it is more efficient to use keyboard techniques to navigate within a table.

To Move	Press This Key
One cell to the right	Tab or Right Arrow
One cell to the left	Shift+Tab or Left Arrow
Down one row	Down Arrow
Up one row	Up Arrow

Add a Row to the Bottom of a Table

As you use the keyboard to navigate in a table, it is possible to inadvertently add a new row to the bottom of the table. Pressing Tab when the insertion point is located in the last cell will add a new row. If you don't want the extra row, simply undo the action.

How to Create a Table

Procedure Reference: Create a Table

To create a table:

1.   Place the insertion point where you want to insert the table.

2.   On the Insert tab, click the Table drop-down arrow.

3.   Insert the table.

   - Insert the table using the grids.

     a.   Move the mouse pointer over the grids to select the desired number of rows and columns to be displayed in the table. Each cell in the grid represents one cell in the table.

     b.   Click to insert the table.

   - Insert the table using the Insert Table dialog box.

     a.   In the Tables group, click Table and select Insert Table.

     b.   In the Insert Table dialog box, type the desired number of rows and columns.

     c.   Click OK to insert the table.

   - Insert the table using the Draw Table option.

     a.   In the Tables group, click Table and select Draw Table.

     b.   Click and drag the pencil-shaped mouse pointer to manually draw the rows and columns.

> If you accidentally insert a table incorrectly, undo the command using the Undo button on the Quick Access toolbar and try again.

4.   Enter the table data.

Add a Tab Character to a Cell

You cannot use the Tab key on the keyboard to insert a tab character into a table, because pressing Tab will move the insertion point to the next cell. To insert a tab within a cell, press Ctrl+Tab.

Type Text Before a Table

When a table is at the beginning of a document, there's no obvious way to type text above the table. The trick is to place the insertion point in the first cell of the first row of the blank table and press Enter. This inserts a paragraph mark above the table. You can then type as much text as you want.

ACTIVITY 5-1

Inserting a Table

Data Files:

Sales Data.docx

Before You Begin

From the C:\084893Data\Adding Tables folder, open Sales Data.docx.

Scenario:

Your manager has supplied you with a document named Sales Data. The data is rather difficult to follow in paragraph form. You decide that the data would work better in table form,
with a row for each salesperson and a column for each of the other pieces of data. You need
to create the table and enter the information.

What You Do	**How You Do It**
1. **Insert a table using the Insert Table dialog box.**	a. **Place the cursor at the end of the document.**
	b. On the Insert tab, in the Tables group, **click Table and select Insert Table.**
	c. In the Number Of Columns text box, **type 3** and **press Tab.**
	d. In the Number Of Rows text box, **type 4**
	e. **Click OK** to close the Insert Table dialog box and create the table.
2. **Enter data in the header row.**	a. In the table, **with the insertion point in the first cell, type Associate and then press Tab.**
	b. **Type Supervisor and press Tab.**
	c. **Type Territory**
3. **Edit the heading.**	a. **Press Shift+Tab twice** to navigate to the cell with the text "Associate".
	b. **Type New Associate** to replace the old heading with the new one.

4. Enter the data for Tim Jones.

a. **Press the Down arrow** to move the insertion point to the first cell in the second row.

b. **Type *Tim Jones* and press Tab.**

c. **Type *Kris Rogers* as the supervisor and press Tab.**

d. **Type *Los Angeles* as the territory and press Tab.**

---

5. Enter the remaining data in the table.

a. Based on the values given in the paragraph above the table, **enter the data for Missy Lu and Miles Rodriguez.**

New Associate	Supervisor	Territory
Tim Jones	Kris Rogers	Los Angeles
Missy Lu	Chris Burke	Seattle
Miles Rodriguez	Cindy Bradley	Boston

b. **Save the document as *My Sales Data.docx* and close it.**

TOPIC B
Modify the Table Structure

You have added a table to your document and entered some data into it. As you work on the table, you may find that it contains more rows than required, or that the cell size needs adjusting. In this topic, you will modify the table structure.

Imagine you've created a table for the third-quarter report that shows the year-to-date revenues for your territory. Then, your manager decides it would be best to include a full year's worth of data and compare it to the same data for another territory. You're going to need extra columns and rows and you might even need to move some of the existing information around. You could start from scratch and create a whole new table structure, but then you would have to re-enter all of your existing information. Instead, you could just take your existing table and modify its structure to meet the new requirements.

Contextual Tabs

Definition:

Contextual tabs are tabs with specialized commands that are displayed when the object that they operate on, such as a table, picture, or shape, is selected. They are displayed along with the core tabs on the Ribbon and are used to modify and format the selected object. The contextual tabs that appear are specific to the type of object that is selected.

Example:

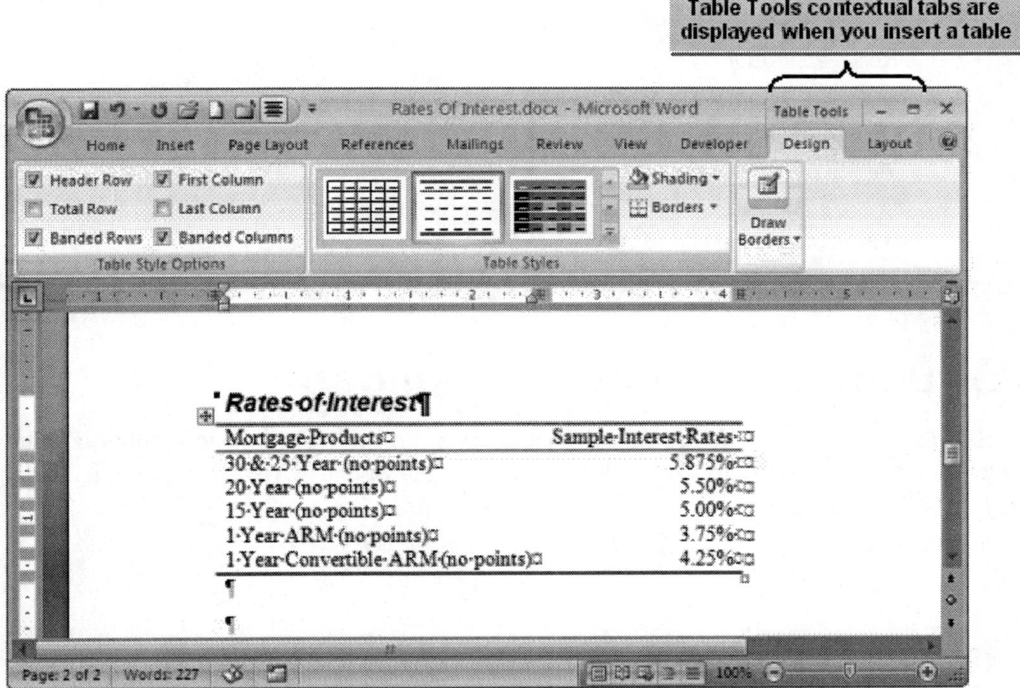

Figure 5-2: Table Tools contextual tabs.

The Table Tools Design Contextual Tab

The Table Tools Design contextual tab contains groups with options to format the table.

Group	Description
Table Style Options	Enables you to format the table by differentiating specified rows or columns.
Table Styles	Provides a set of predefined styles to format a table. Also enables adding a different shading and applying borders to the table.
Draw Borders	Enables you to draw borders to your table. This group contains options to change the line style, color, and thickness of the border. You can also erase the border.

The Table Tools Layout Contextual Tab

The Table Tools Layout contextual tab contains groups with options to modify the layout of the table.

Group	Provides options to:
Table	Selects a particular table or cells of a table, shows or hide gridlines, and displays the table properties.
Rows & Columns	Modifies the table structure by inserting or deleting rows or columns.
Merge	Merges or splits tables and cells.
Cell Size	Resizes the table.
Alignment	Modifies the alignment of text inside the table. This group contains options to change the direction in which text has been entered. You can also change the default value of each cell's margins.
Data	Sorts, calculates, or converts the table information into text. You can also use options in this group to repeat heading information on every page.

Table Structure Modification Options

You might need to modify the structure of an existing table to include more information or to delete unnecessary information from the cells. You can delete or insert rows or columns, move cells, rows, or columns, or change the overall size of the table.

The Table Properties Dialog Box

You can click Properties in the Table group of the Table Tools Layout contextual tab to open the Table Properties dialog box and specify settings for rows, columns, individual cells, or the entire table.

Tab	Provides options to:
Table	Sets the size, alignment, and text wrapping of the table.
Row	Sets the height. This tab also allows you to apply a page break and navigate to the previous or next row.
Column	Modifies the size of the selected column. This tab also allows you to navigate to the previous or the next column.
Cell	Modifies the size and the vertical alignment of the selected cell.

How to Modify Table Structure

Procedure Reference: Insert Rows or Columns

To insert rows or columns:

1. Position the insertion point next to where you want to insert or delete the columns or rows. To insert multiple columns or rows, select that number of existing rows or columns in the table.

2. Select the Table Tools Layout contextual tab.

3. Insert the columns or rows.

   - In the Rows & Columns group, click Insert Left or Insert Right to insert a column to the left or right of the selected column.

   - In the Rows & Columns group, click Insert Above or Insert Below to insert a row above or below the selected row.

   - Select the last cell of the table and press Tab to insert a row at the bottom of the table.

Table Selection Methods

There are many selection techniques you can use to select the components of a table that you want to work with.

To Select	Do This
A row or rows	Move the mouse pointer in the blank space to the left of the desired row and when the pointer changes to a right-tilted white arrow, click to select the row. You can also click and drag to the left of the table to select several rows.
A column or columns	Move the mouse pointer at the top or bottom line border of the column until the mouse pointer changes to a down-headed arrow and click to select the column. You can also click and drag above the table to select several columns.

To Select	Do This
A cell or cells	Move the mouse pointer in the blank space before the text in a cell and when the mouse pointer changes to a right-tilted dark arrow, click to select the cell. To select a group of cells, drag over the cells, or click a cell, hold Shift, and click the last cell.
The entire table	Point to the table until the table selection box appears to the top left of the table, and then click the box. Or, on the Layout tab in the Table group, click Select and select Select Table.

Procedure Reference: Delete Rows or Columns

To delete rows or column:

1. Position the insertion point in the desired column or row. To delete multiple rows or columns, select them as a group.

2. Delete the columns or rows.

   - On the Table Tools Layout contextual tab, in the Rows & Columns group, click Delete and select Delete Columns or Delete Rows.

   - Or, right-click and choose Delete Cells, select Delete Entire Column or Delete Entire Row, and click OK.

Inserting or Deleting Cells

You can insert individual cells by going to the Table Tools Layout contextual tab and clicking the Insert Cells Dialog Box Launcher button in the Rows & Columns group or by right-clicking and selecting Insert Cells from the Insert submenu. When you do so, you can shift the existing cells down in the current columns or to the right in the current rows.

You can delete individual cells by clicking Delete and selecting Delete Cells. When you do so, you can shift the existing cells up in the current columns or to the left in the current rows.

Procedure Reference: Move Columns or Rows

To move columns or rows:

1. Select the columns or rows to move.

2. Click the Cut button, or right-click the selection and click Cut.

3. Place the insertion point to the right of the existing column or below the existing row where you want to paste the content.

4. Click the Paste button, or right-click and choose Paste Columns or Paste Rows.

Moving Cells

You cannot move individual cells by cutting and pasting. Instead, when you paste cells, Word replaces the contents of the target cells.

Procedure Reference: Set Column Width or Row Height

To set column width or row height:

1. Place the insertion point inside the row or column, or select multiple rows or columns.

2. On the Table Tools Layout contextual tab, in the Table group, click Properties.

3. Set a specific column width.

   a. Select the Column tab.

   b. In the Size section, check the Preferred Width check box.

   c. In the Preferred Width spin box, specify the desired column width using the up and down arrows.

   d. Click the Previous Column or Next Column button to change the width of the previous or next column.

4. To set a specific row height, select the Row tab and follow a similar procedure.

5. Click OK to close the Table Properties dialog box.

6. To set an approximate row height or column width, click and drag the row or column border.

7. To fit the row height or column width to the contents of the cells, double-click the right column boundary or the top row boundary.

ACTIVITY 5-2
Modify Table Structure

Data Files:

Mortgage Letter.docx

Before You Begin

From the C:\084893Data\Adding Tables folder, open Mortgage Letter.docx.

Scenario:

As you are preparing your mortgage rates letter, the client calls and reminds you that the company he works for is opening a branch office in Rochester, New York later in the year and that he might possibly be transferred to that location. He would like you to include specific information on loan rates for Rochester. You also realize that the information on the rate percentage is more important to your customer than the effective date. Also, the columns of the table look too large, so you decide to modify the column width within the table.

What You Do	How You Do It
1. Insert an additional row into the table.	a. In the table, **click at the beginning of the cell that contains "Seattle, WA".**
	b. **Click the Table Tools Layout contextual tab.**
	c. In the Rows & Columns group, **click Insert Above.**
2. Enter data in the new row.	a. In the new row, in the first cell, **type** *Rochester, NY* **and press Tab.**
	b. In the second cell, **type** *July 8* **and press Tab.**
	c. In the last cell, **type** *6.13*

<table>
<tr><td>3.</td><td>Reverse the order of the last two columns.</td><td>a.</td><td>In the table, move the mouse pointer above the border of the "Rate" column and when the mouse pointer changes to a down-headed arrow, click to select the column.</td></tr>
<tr><td></td><td></td><td>b.</td><td>On the Home tab, in the Clipboard group, click the Cut button.</td></tr>
<tr><td></td><td></td><td>c.</td><td>Verify that the insertion point is in the "As of" column heading.</td></tr>
<tr><td></td><td></td><td>d.</td><td>In the Clipboard group, click the Paste button.</td></tr>
</table>

<table>
<tr><td>4.</td><td>Adjust the column width to fit the contents.</td><td>a.</td><td>In the table, position the mouse pointer anywhere on the right border of the "Location" column and double-click when the mouse pointer changes to a double-headed arrow to adjust the width of the column to fit its contents.</td></tr>
<tr><td></td><td></td><td>b.</td><td>Double-click the border left to the Location column, to adjust the width of the Rate and As Of columns.</td></tr>
</table>

Location¤	Rate·(%)¤	As·of:¤	¤
Los·Angeles,·CA¤	6.73¤	July·11¤	¤
Denver,·CO¤	6.82¤	July·9¤	¤
Washington,·DC¤	6.63¤	July·15¤	¤
Miami,·FL¤	6.79¤	July·12¤	¤
Atlanta,·GA¤	6.75¤	July·9¤	¤
Chicago,·IL¤	6.96¤	July·11¤	¤
Boston,·MA¤	6.77¤	July·15¤	¤
New·York,·NY¤	6.86¤	July·6¤	¤
Philadelphia,·PA¤	6.71¤	July·12¤	¤
Rochester,·NY¤	6.13¤	July·8¤	¤
Seattle,·WA¤	6.77¤	July·13¤	¤

<table>
<tr><td></td><td></td><td>c.</td><td>Save the file as My Mortgage Letter.docx and close the file.</td></tr>
</table>

TOPIC C
Format a Table

In the previous topic, you adjusted the structure of a table to match the data you need to present. Once the table's data and structure are established, all you need to do to complete your table is to format it. In this topic, you will quickly format a table, applying a variety of formatting options all at the same time.

A simple table can effectively organize information logically. However, if you were to insert a plain table within an otherwise formatted document, the table might not match the overall look of the document and might not draw the reader's attention. You know that the right combination of formats can make the information stand out. To make it easy to achieve the right look, Word enables you to select from an existing set of pre-formatted table designs and apply them automatically to your table.

Table Styles

Definition:

A *table style* is a formatting option that contains a group of table-specific formatting options packaged together to apply design and formatting changes to an existing table all at the same time. Table formatting options include borders, shading, colors, cell alignment, table fonts, and separate formats for the first column or row. In the Table Tools Design contextual tab, you can select a style from the Table Styles gallery within the Table Styles group. You can also modify an existing style, or build a new style and add it to the Styles gallery.

Example:

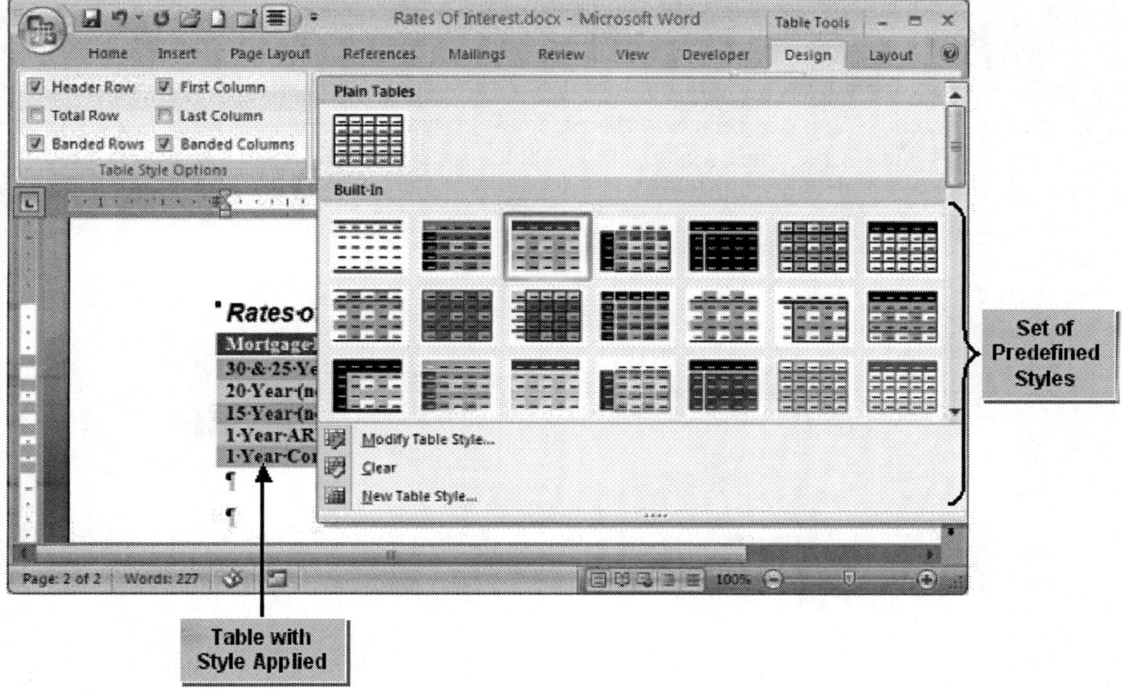

Figure 5-3: Table Styles.

The Table Style Options Group

The Table Style Options group contains options to differentiate the contents of the table based on the location of the respective rows and columns. You can apply separate formats to the header, or first row; the totals, or last row; and the first and last columns. You can also select banded rows or banded columns, in which alternate rows or columns appear in a contrasting shade.

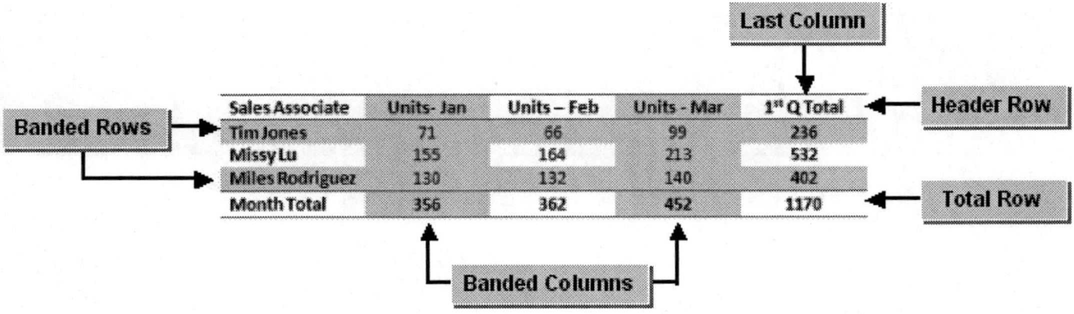

Sales Associate	Units- Jan	Units – Feb	Units - Mar	1st Q Total
Tim Jones	71	66	99	236
Missy Lu	155	164	213	532
Miles Rodriguez	130	132	140	402
Month Total	356	362	452	1170

Figure 5-4: Sections of a table with table style options applied.

Quick Tables

Definition:

Quick Tables are predefined tables with a style applied and sample data entered into the cells. You can use a Quick Table to quickly insert a new table with a pre-defined format rather than a plain grid of squares. You can then edit the placeholder text in the Quick Table to suit your needs. In Word, Quick Tables are located in the Tables group on the Insert tab. There are different types of Quick Tables including calendars, double tables, and tables with subheadings. Quick Tables may apply a coordinated set of different fonts and column delimiters to your table.

Example:

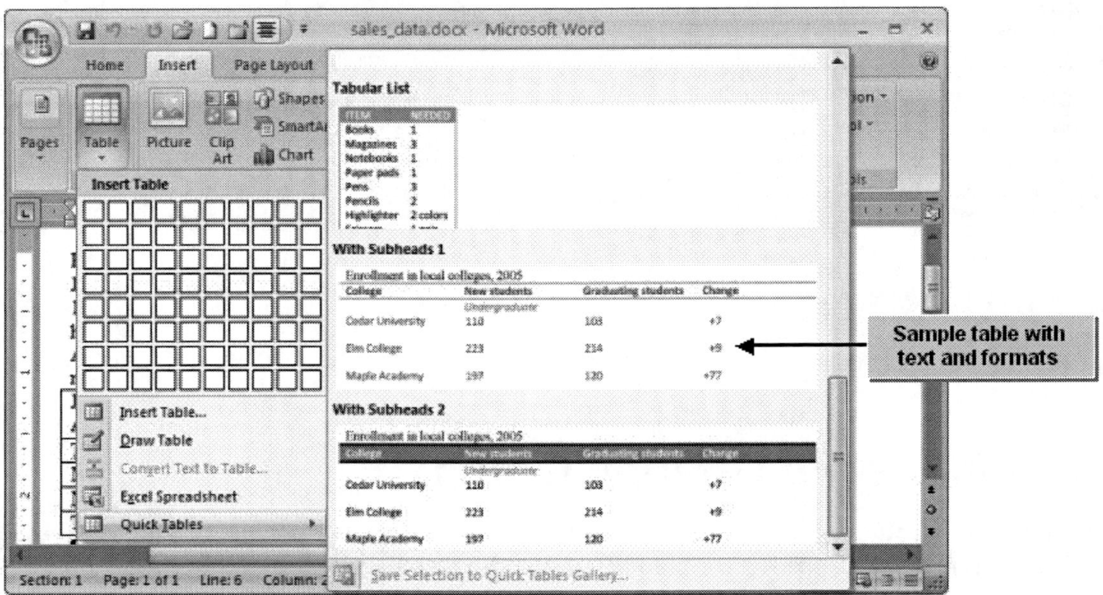

Figure 5-5: *Quick Tables.*

 To format an existing table, use a table style. To insert a new formatted table, use a Quick Table.

How to Format a Table

Procedure Reference: Use a Quick Table to Create a Formatted Table

To use a Quick Table to create a formatted table:

1. On the Insert tab, in the Tables group, click Table and select Quick Tables.
2. In the Quick Tables gallery, select a pre-defined table.
3. In the table, replace the existing data with the data you want to display in the table.

Procedure Reference: Format Using Contextual Tabs

To format a table using contextual tabs:

1. Select the table.
2. To format the entire table, in the Table Styles group of the Table Tools Design contextual tab, from the Table Styles gallery, select a style.
3. To format a section of a table, select the section and apply the format.
   - Select a row or column and select the desired option in the Table Style Options group.
   - To apply shading, in the Table Styles group, click Shading and select the desired color.
   - To apply borders, in the Table Styles group, click the Borders drop-down arrow and select the desired border. You can also draw in the borders or erase existing borders by using the options in the Draw Borders group.

ACTIVITY 5-3

Formatting a Table

Scenario:

Your colleague is going to provide you with a handwritten list of the four branches with the highest sales percentages last year. You will need to include this data in several documents, and you think it would look best if it were in a table. You want to create and format the table as quickly as possible so that you will be ready to enter the data when you receive it.

What You Do	How You Do It
1. Insert a Quick Table.	a. **Open a new, blank document.**
	b. On the Insert tab, in the Tables group, **click Table and select Quick Tables.**
	c. In the Quick Tables gallery, **scroll down and select Tabular List** to insert that Quick Table.

ITEM¤	NEEDED¤	¤
Books¤	1¤	¤
Magazines¤	3¤	¤
Notebooks¤	1¤	¤
Paper·pads¤	1¤	¤
Pens¤	3¤	¤
Pencils¤	2¤	¤
Highlighter¤	2·colors¤	¤
Scissors¤	1·pair¤	¤

¶

What You Do	How You Do It
2. Apply a style to the table.	a. **Verify that the mouse pointer is at the beginning of the table and select the table.**
	b. On the Table Tools Design contextual tab, in the Table Styles group, **click the More button.**

c. In the Table Styles gallery, in the Built-In section, in the first row, **select the second style, Light Shading-Accent 1.**

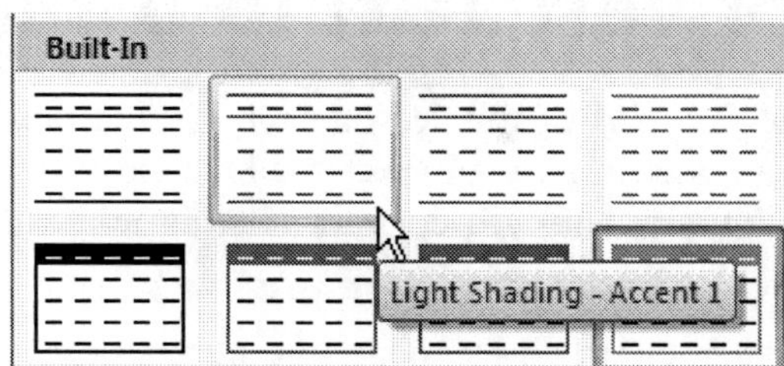

d. **Click in any cell** to deselect the table.

e. In the Table Style Options group, **check the Banded Rows check box.**

ITEM¤	NEEDED¤	¤
Books¤	1¤	¤
Magazines¤	3¤	¤
Notebooks¤	1¤	¤
Paper·pads¤	1¤	¤
Pens¤	3¤	¤
Pencils¤	2¤	¤
Highlighter¤	2·colors¤	¤
Scissors¤	1·pair¤	¤

3. **Edit the content of the default table.**

a. In the table, **double-click the word ITEM and type** *City*

b. **Double-click the word NEEDED and type** *Percent*

c. **Select the remaining rows of the table and press Delete** to clear the contents of the cells.

d. **Select the last four rows of the table.**

e. On the Table Tools Contextual tab, in the Rows & Columns group, **click Delete and select Delete Rows.**

f. **Save the document as** *My Sales Table.docx* **and close the document.**

TOPIC D

Convert Text to a Table or Tables to Text

In the first part of this lesson, you created tables manually. In some instances, you might have data already in a document, in which case it could be time-consuming to retype it into a table. In this topic, you will convert existing text into a new table, as well as convert tables back to text.

You've been asked to update the new product catalog sheet. The person who originally created the document in Word didn't know how to create a table, so he used tabs instead. The information would certainly be more readable if it were put into a formatted table. But, since the document is several pages long, it would take a long time to retype and format all the information in a new table, not to mention you may make mistakes as you type. However, Word can quickly convert the existing tabbed text into a table, without the risk of mistakes, and you can format the table at the same time.

The Convert Text To Table Dialog Box

If you have used tab characters to create columns of data in your document, you can convert the tabbed text to a table by using options in the Convert Text To Table dialog box.

Conversion Options	Description
Table Size	Enables you to modify the number of rows and columns to suit the text content.
AutoFit Behavior	Provides options to automatically resize the table based on the content, window or the width of the columns.
Separate Text At	Provides options to specify whether paragraphs, tabs, commas, or any other option should be considered as the delimiter to separate text while converting the text to a table.

Comma-separated data is a common data format used by both government and industry.

The Convert Table To Text Dialog Box

You can use the Convert Table To Text dialog box to convert information in a table to paragraph format. This dialog box can be accessed from the Data group in the Table Tools Layout contextual tab. The dialog box provides options to separate the data in the table using paragraph marks, tabs, commas, or other delimiting characters when it is converted into text.

How to Convert Text to a Table or Tables to Text

Procedure Reference: Convert Text to a Table Using the Convert Text To Table Dialog Box

To convert text to a table using the Text To Table dialog box:

1. Select the text that you want to convert into a table.

It's helpful to have non-printing characters displayed so you can see the tabs, because, if you have extra tabs in the text, they will be converted into empty cells when the table is created. Click the Show/Hide button to display non-printing characters.

2. On the Insert tab, in the Tables group, click Table and select Convert Text To Table.
3. In the Convert Text To Table dialog box, set the Table properties.
    *   In the Table Size section, specify the desired number of rows and columns using the up and down arrows in the spin box.
    *   In the AutoFit Behavior section, select the options to automatically modify the size of the rows and columns to suit the content.
        *   Select Fixed Column Width to maintain a fixed column width or modify the column width using the up and down arrow in the Fixed Column Width spin box.
        *   Select AutoFit To Contents to automatically fit the data to a table.
        *   Select AutoFit To Window to automatically fit the table to the window.
    *   In the Separate Text At section, select an option to set the delimiter character.
4. Click OK to insert the table.

Procedure Reference: Convert a Table to Text Using the Convert Table To Text Dialog Box

To convert a table to text using the Convert Table To Text dialog box:

1. Select the desired table.
2. On the Table Tools Layout contextual tab, in the Data group, click Convert To Text.
3. In the Convert Table To Text dialog box, select the desired option to set a delimiter for the data after converting it to text.
4. Click OK to convert the table to text.

ACTIVITY 5-4

Converting Tabbed Text into a Table

Data Files:

Burke Review.docx

Before You Begin

From the C:\084893Data\Adding Tables folder, open Burke Review.docx.

Scenario:

Your coworker has asked you to help her with the Burke Review document. She has used tabs to separate data in the document. You want to make the data more readable without spending much time on it, so you decide to convert the tabbed text into a table.

What You Do	How You Do It
1. Convert tabbed text into a basic table.	a. In the second paragraph, **select the tabbed text "Tim Jones" through "translates into sales."**

Junior·Sales·Associate·Performance·Review¶
After·sluggish·sales·in·the·first·two·months·of·the·quarter,·all·three·junior·sales·associates·showed·marked·improvements.·Much·of·the·difficulties·they·faced·were·seasonal.·(Post-holiday/winter·sales·are·typically·weak.)·The·junior·sales·associate·summary·follows:¶

Tim·Jones → Had·a·very·tough·month·in·February.·However·he·showed·a·strong·improvement·in·March.·Recommend·continued·mentoring·with·a·senior·associate.¶
Missy·Lu → By·far·the·most·consistent·sales·associate.·Her·sales·remained·strong·despite·seasonal·hurdles.·Recommend·promotion·at·first·opportunity.¶
Miles·Rodriguez → Shows·steady·sales,·but·seems·unmotivated.·Recommend·testing·the·new·incentive·programs·on·him·to·see·if·that·translates·into·sales.¶

b. On the Insert tab, in the Tables group, **click Table and select Insert Table.**

c. **Click away from the table** to deselect it.

Tim·Jones	Had·a·very·tough·month·in·February.·However·he·showed·a·strong·improvement·in·March.·Recommend·continued·mentoring·with·a·senior·associate.
Missy·Lu	By·far·the·most·consistent·sales·associate.·Her·sales·remained·strong·despite·seasonal·hurdles.·Recommend·promotion·at·first·opportunity.
Miles·Rodriguez	Shows·steady·sales,·but·seems·unmotivated.·Recommend·testing·the·new·incentive·programs·on·him·to·see·if·that·translates·into·sales.

2. Convert the second block of tabbed data into a table that fits the contents exactly.

a. At the bottom of the document, **select the tabbed data, "Jr. Sales Associate" through the last "3".**

b. On the Insert tab, in the Tables group, **click Table and select Convert Text To Table.**

c. In the Convert Text To Table dialog box, **verify that the table has four columns, and select the AutoFit To Contents option.**

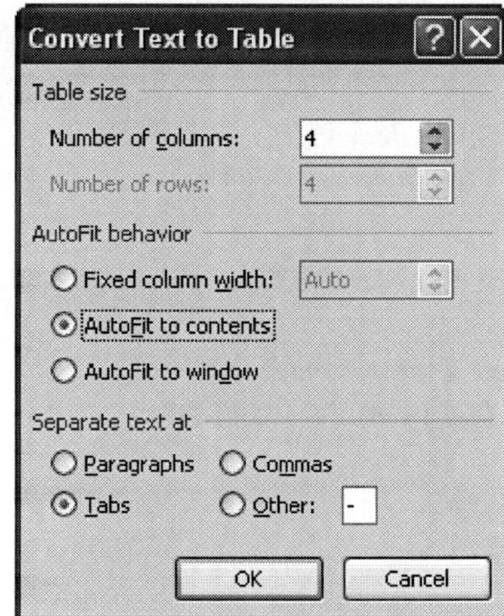

d. **Click OK** to convert the tabbed text into a formatted table.

e. **Click away from the table** to deselect the text in the table.

Jr. Sales Associate	Jan	Feb	Mar	
Tim Jones	6	1	5	
Missy Lu	5	6	6	
Miles Rodriguez	3	4	3	

f. **Save the document as** *My Burke Review.docx* **and close it.**

ACTIVITY 5-5

Converting an Existing Table to Text

Data Files:

Rates of Interest.docx

Before You Begin

From the C:\084893Data\Adding Tables folder, open Rates of Interest.docx.

Scenario:

As you review the document, you find that the information does not require a table and is more readable when presented in a paragraph format.

What You Do	How You Do It
1. Convert a table to text, with paragraph marks as the delimiter.	a. At the beginning of the document, **select the "Points Of Interest" table.**
	b. On the Table Tools Layout contextual tab, in the Data group, **click Convert To Text.**
	c. In the Convert Table To Text dialog box, **verify that the Paragraph Marks option is selected and click OK.**
	d. **Click in the text area** to deselect the text.
	Points·of·Interest:¶ Interest·rates·seem·to·be·rising,·as·a·result·of·an·improving·stock·market.¶ The·Federal·Reserve·Bank·is·discussing·methods·that·can·be·used·to·help·first-time·homebuyers.·Such·methods·may·include·discounted·rates·and·removing·IRA·penalties.¶ The·Northeast·still·has·the·highest·interest·rates·on·a·national·basis.¶
2. Save the document.	a. **Save the file as *My Rates Of Interest.docx* and close it.**

Lesson 5 Follow-up

In this lesson, you created a table, entered data, and modified the table structure to suit your content. You also formatted the table to enhance the appearance. Lastly, you converted the existing tabbed-text into its own table. Tables can significantly improve reader comprehension by enabling you to organize your information more clearly.

1.   **When will you use tables in your documents?**

2.   **What type of information will you put in tables?**

6 | Inserting Graphic Objects

Lesson Time: 30 minutes

Lesson Objectives:

In this lesson, you will add graphic elements to a document.

You will:

- Insert symbols and special characters.
- Insert illustrations.

Introduction

You have been working with text and tables in documents. Now, you want to insert graphic elements into your document to create a visual impact. In this lesson, you will enhance the visual appeal of your documents by adding graphic elements to them.

When you create a large document with pages of only text, it can be difficult to read, follow, and understand. By inserting graphical objects, you can engage the readers and ensure better comprehension of content.

TOPIC A

Add Visual Effects Using Symbols and Special Characters

In this lesson, you will insert graphic objects into documents. Some of the simplest and most common graphic objects that occur in all types of documents are basic symbols and special characters such as the copyright symbol (©). In this topic, you will add visual effects using symbols and special characters.

You are drafting a copyright statement and the new department style guide requires that you use the copyright symbol (©) along with the word "copyright." You've stared at your keyboard for several minutes trying to locate the character, but it's nowhere to be found. How are you going to get the circle around the letter "c"? You know it can be done, but how? Word provides convenient access to a large group of symbols and special characters, such as the copyright character, that can be inserted quickly and correctly.

Symbols

Symbols are character marks included with a font that can be used to represent an idea or word such as copyright, trademark, or registered trademark. Each font can have a slightly different set of symbols. Click the Symbol option in the Symbols group on the Insert tab to insert symbols from the Symbol gallery. You can also click More Symbols to open the Symbol dialog box to insert or manage symbols.

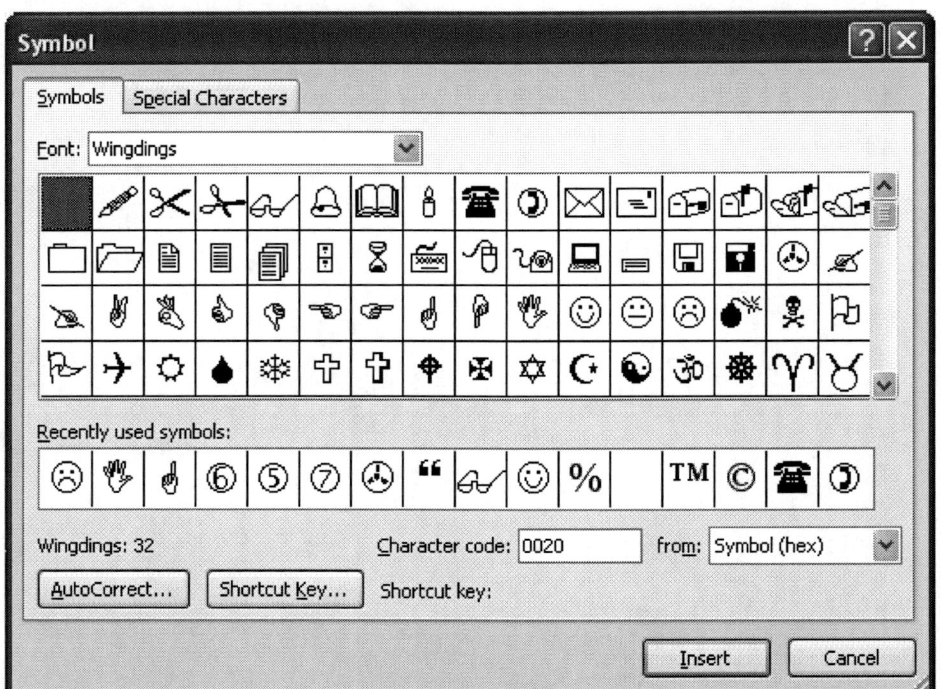

Figure 6-1: *Options on the Symbols tab.*

Symbol Families and Character Codes

In the Symbols dialog box, you can choose symbols from two different standard symbol families: ASCII (American Standard Code for Information Interchange) standard symbols or Unicode standard symbols. These are both standards that enable computers to communicate information by representing letters as numeric values. For each symbol in each family, there is a character code in decimal or hexadecimal format that you can use to enter the character from the keyboard or numeric keypad. The Unicode (hex) symbol family is broken down into subsets; you can use the Subset drop-down list to choose which subset to display to make it easier for you to scroll and locate a particular symbol.

Special Characters

Special characters are punctuation, spacing, or typographical characters that typically are not available on the standard keyboard. The Special Characters tab in the Symbol dialog box allows you to access these characters and commonly used symbols such as Trademark, Registered, and Copyright.

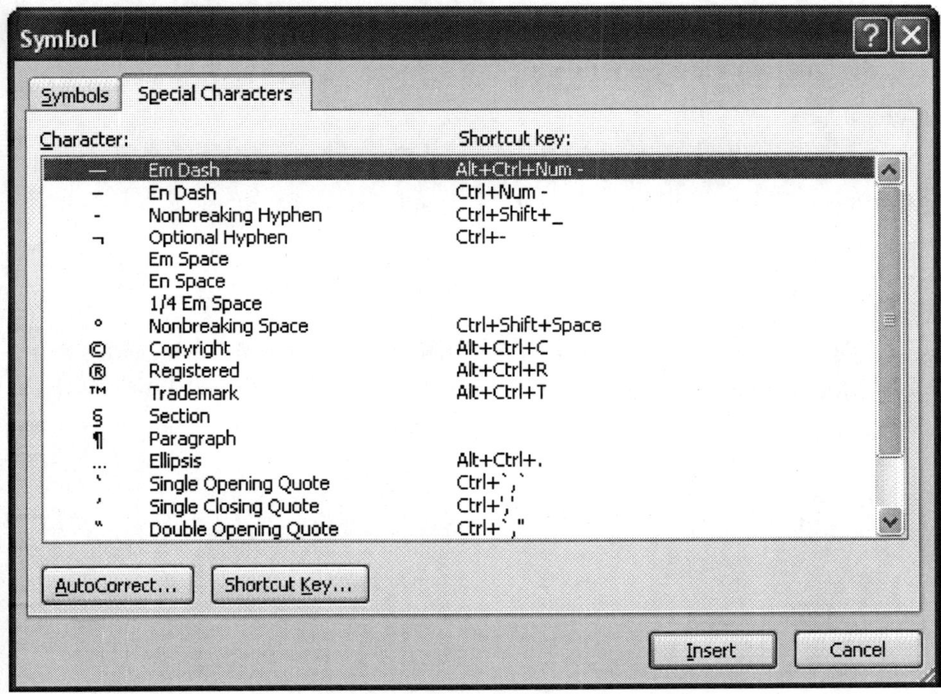

Figure 6-2: Options on the Special Characters tab.

How to Insert Symbols and Special Characters

Procedure Reference: Insert a Symbol or Special Character

To insert a symbol or special character:

1. Place the insertion point where you want to insert the symbol or special character.

2. Insert a symbol.

   - On the Insert tab, in the Symbols group, click Symbol and select the symbol from the Symbols gallery.

   - Or, insert the symbol using the Symbol dialog box.

     a. On the Insert tab, in the Symbols group, click Symbol.

     b. In the Symbol gallery, click More Symbols to display the Symbol dialog box.

     c. On the Symbols tab, from the Font drop-down list, select the font that includes the symbol you want to use.

     d. In the Symbols palette, select a symbol and click Insert, or double-click a symbol to directly insert it.

     e. Click Close to close the Symbol dialog box.

3. Insert a special character.

   a. Open the Symbol dialog box and select the Special Characters tab.

   b. Select the desired character and click Insert, or double-click the character.

   c. Click Close.

The Wingdings Font

Wingdings is a font available in Word that includes many decorative symbols. Wingdings represent some common computer components and other elements of graphical user interfaces.

ACTIVITY 6-1

Inserting Symbols and Special Characters

Data Files:

Rates of Interest.docx

Before You Begin

From the C:\084893Data\Inserting Graphic Objects folder, open Rates of Interest.docx.

Scenario:

You've finished drafting a company newsletter called "Rates of Interest." In the Legal Information text, the company style guide requires a registered trademark character immediately following the "Rates of Interest" publication name and a copyright character between the word "copyright" and the year that the document was published. Furthermore, the style guide requires that the word "Phone" be replaced by a Wingdings telephone symbol in the "Contact Information" text.

What You Do	How You Do It
1. Insert the Registered special character.	a. In the second to last line of the "Legal Information" paragraph, **place the insertion point after the italicized word "Interest".**
	b. On the Insert tab, in the Symbols group, **click Symbol.**
	c. In the Symbols gallery, **click More Symbols.**
	d. In the Symbol dialog box, **select the Special Characters tab.**
	e. In the Character list box, **select Registered.**

©	Copyright	Alt+Ctrl+C
®	Registered	Alt+Ctrl+R
™	Trademark	Alt+Ctrl+T

f. **Click Insert and then click Close.**

2. **Insert a Copyright symbol.**

   a. In the same paragraph, **position the insertion point before "2007".**

   b. In the Symbols group, **click Symbol.**

   c. In the Symbol gallery, **click the Copyright Sign symbol.**

3. **Replace the word "Phone" with a Wingdings telephone symbol.**

   a. Under "Contact Information", **select the word "Phone".**

   b. In the Symbols group, **click Symbol and select More Symbols.**

   c. In the Symbol dialog box, **click the Font drop-down arrow and press W** to view all the fonts that begin with W.

   d. **Select Wingdings** to view the set of symbols for this font.

   e. In the first row, **select the Telephone icon.**

   f. **Click Insert and then click Close.**

   g. **Save the document as *My Rates of Interest.docx***

TOPIC B

Insert Illustrations

You are not limited to inserting just text symbols and special characters to add visual interest to your documents. Word comes with a wide variety of colorful graphics you can use to illustrate text. In this topic, you will enhance documents by adding illustrations to them.

You've added as much text formatting as you can without it becoming a distraction, yet your document still needs something. You would like to insert a simple image in the document to support the text's message. Word provides an extensive catalog of professionally created pictures that you can add to your documents to make them more memorable.

Illustrations

Definition:

Illustrations are graphics or media elements that you can insert into documents to provide visual representations of text or add visual interest to the document. Illustrations can be static graphics such as clip art, geometric shapes, pictures, or charts, or they can be embedded media files such as movies or audio recordings. After you insert illustrations, you can resize them, move them, and adjust their appearance in your document.

Example:

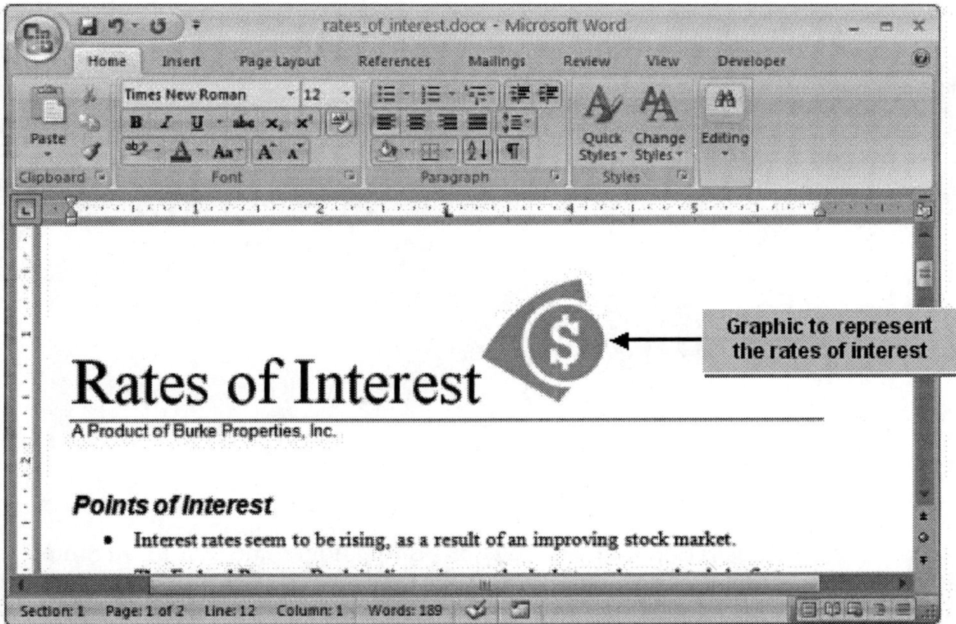

Figure 6-3: An illustration.

SmartArt

SmartArt is a graphic element that combines text, illustration, and color. It is used to show a timeline or developmental progression. SmartArt can also represent the sequential steps in a process or workflow. SmartArt is highly customizable to suit your exact information needs.

Charts

A chart is a graphical representation of statistical data. It is used to form a relationship between different groups of data. There are different types of charts such as Bar, Pie, and Line.

Pictures

Definition:

A *picture* is a type of illustration that closely resembles a real object. In Word, pictures can be digital renderings of paintings, digital photographs, or computer graphics. They are stored in files that use a graphic format such as .jpg, .gif, or .bmp. Pictures can be any size or shape.

Example:

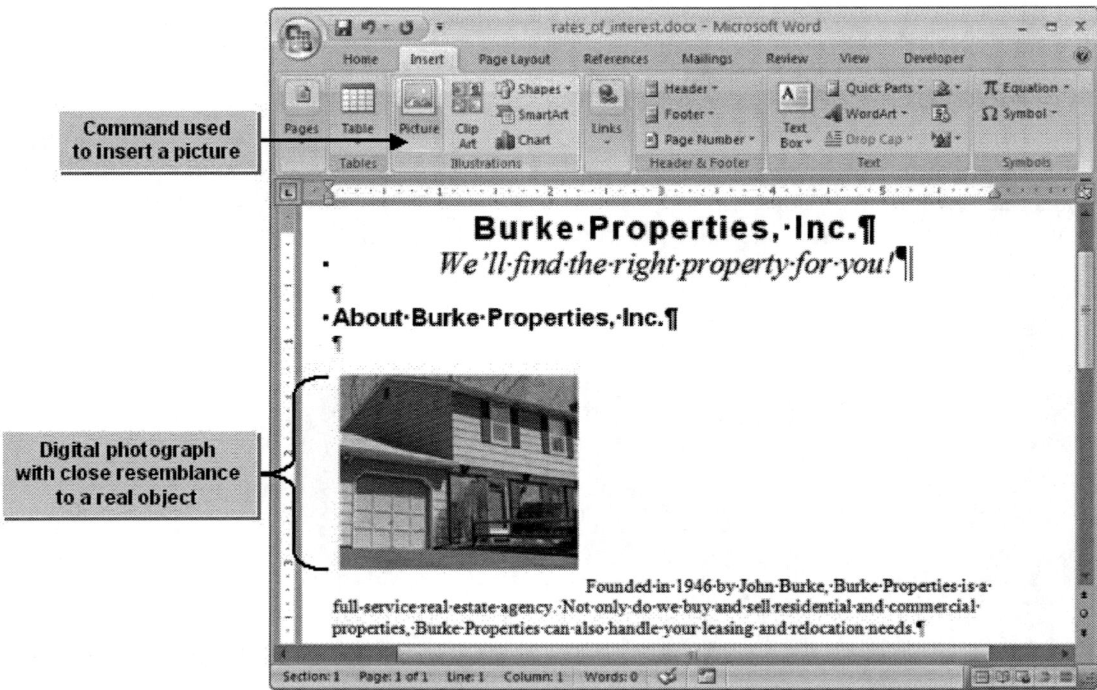

Figure 6-4: A digital photograph used as a picture.

Clip Art

Definition:

A *clip art* image is a type of illustration that generally is non-photographic and has a simple two-dimensional effect. Word includes a number of default Clip Art images, and you can use the Clip Art task pane in the Illustrations group to search for additional Clip Art as well as other types of illustrations.

Example:

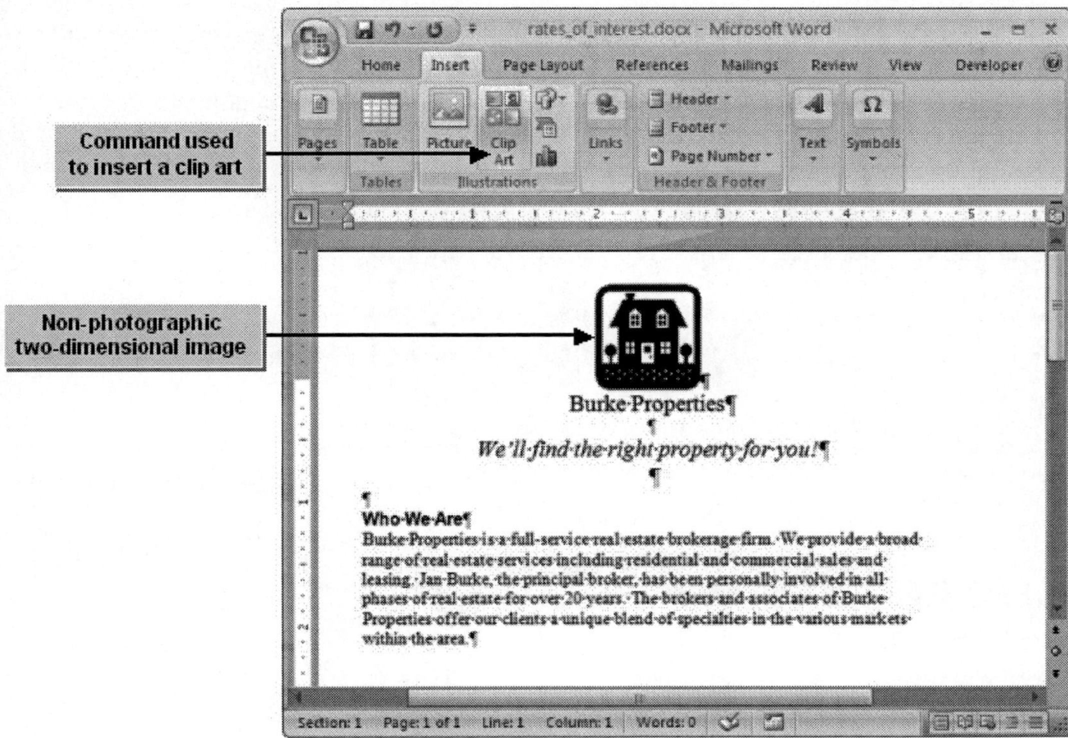

Figure 6-5: Clip art inserted into a Word document.

The Illustrations Group

The Illustrations group on the Insert tab contains options you can use to insert pictures or clip art, as well as other types of illustrations such as geometric shapes, SmartArt, and charts. Click Picture to open the Insert Picture dialog box to locate and insert pictures. Click Clip Art to display the Clip Art task pane where you can search for clip art and other media types.

The Clip Art Task Pane

The Clip Art task pane is used to search for media files or clips of various types that are stored on your computer and the web. You can search for clip art, photographs, movies, and sound files by entering a word or phrase that describes the clip you want to find. You can also use the Clip Art task pane to open the Microsoft Clip Organizer to arrange your Clip Art and other media files, and to access Office Online to download additional clips.

Clip Art Properties

To view a clip's properties, such as its file name, file size, creation date, or search keywords associated with the clip, or if you'd like to preview a clip, move your mouse pointer over the clip's thumbnail and then click the arrow that appears. Choose Preview/Properties to open the Preview/Properties dialog box, where you can preview the clip art and view its properties.

Sizing Techniques

When you select an illustration in a document, small circles and squares called *sizing handles* are displayed around the border of the clip. You can drag the square sizing handles to the left or to the right of the illustration, which resizes the illustration in the direction you drag the handle. Dragging the corner circular sizing handles proportionally resizes the illustration, while the diagonally opposite corner remains fixed. If you hold Ctrl while you drag the corner, you can resize the illustration around its center.

Figure 6-6: *Sizing handles displayed around an image.*

The Picture Tools Format Contextual Tab

Groups on the Picture Tools Format contextual tab enable you to control the appearance of illustrations in the document.

Group	Description
Adjust	Enables you to make formatting changes to images by increasing or decreasing the color, brightness, or contrast.
Picture Styles	Enables you to select a style, shape, border, and effects for a picture.
Arrange	Enables you to position the image in the document. You can also rotate, group, or align pictures within a page using the options in this group.
Size	Enables you to crop the image and to increase or decrease the height and width of the picture.

How to Insert Illustrations

Procedure Reference: Insert a Picture from a File

To insert a picture from a file:

1.   Position the insertion point where you want to insert the picture.
2.   On the Insert tab, in the Illustrations group, click Picture.
3.   In the Insert Picture dialog box, navigate to the folder where the picture is saved.
4.   Select the picture and click Insert to insert the picture in the document.
5.   If desired, click and drag the sizing handles to adjust the picture size.

Procedure Reference: Insert Clip Art

To insert a clip art image:

1.   Position the insertion point where you want to insert the clip art image.
2.   On the Insert tab, in the Illustrations group, click Clip Art.
3.   In the Clip Art task pane, in the Search For text box, type a word or phrase that describes the clip art image you want to locate.
4.   If necessary, narrow down the search.
     - From the Search In drop-down list, select the search locations.
     - From the Results Should Be drop-down list, specify the types of media files you want to find.
5.   Click Go to begin the search.
6.   In the section where clip art is displayed, click a clip to insert it where the insertion point is placed.
7.   If desired, drag the sizing handles to adjust the clip's size.

ACTIVITY 6-2

Inserting Illustrations

Data Files:

Burke Logo.png

Before You Begin

My Rates of Interest.docx is open.

Scenario:

Since the My Rates Of Interest document is going to be a monetary guide frequently used by your coworkers and their clients, you want the document to be instantly identifiable. You decide to add a company logo and a simple money-oriented picture to the top of the document to help accomplish that.

What You Do	How You Do It
1. Insert the Burke Properties logo.	a. **Place the insertion point at the beginning of the heading "Rates of Interest".**
	b. On the Insert tab, in the Illustrations group, **click Picture.**
	c. In the Insert Picture dialog box, **navigate to C:\084893Data\Inserting Graphic Objects.**
	d. **Select Burke Logo.png and click Insert.**
	e. **Click anywhere in the text area** to deselect the image.
2. Align the picture to the center of the document.	a. **Place the insertion point before the words "Rates of Interest" and press Enter twice** to add a blank line between the picture and the heading.
	b. **Click the picture** to select it.
	c. On the Home tab, in the Paragraph group, **click the Center button** to align the picture to the center.

3. **Search for clip art pictures related to money.**

   a. **Place the insertion point at the end of the heading "Rates of Interest".**

   b. On the Insert tab, in the Illustrations group, **click Clip Art** to display the Clip Art task pane.

   c. In the Search For text box, **type *money***

   d. To limit the search to clip art, **click the Results Should Be drop-down arrow and uncheck the Photographs, Movies, and Sounds check boxes.**

   e. **Click Go** to display all the clip art related to money.

   f. In the Microsoft Clip Organizer message box, **click No.**

4. **Insert and resize the yellow dollar sign clip art image.**

   a. In the Results area of the Clip Art task pane, **click the yellow-orange dollar sign clip art image** to insert it into the document.

   b. **Drag the top-right corner sizing handle diagonally downward until the picture is about an inch square.**

   c. **Click anywhere in the blank area** to deselect the clip art image.

   d. **Close the Clip Art task pane.**

   e. **Save the document and close it.**

Lesson 6 Follow-up

In this lesson, you added graphic elements to enhance a document. With these enhancements, you will be able to add interest and visual appeal to the output of many types of Word documents.

1. **What are some symbols and special characters that you find useful to use in your documents?**

2. **What is your opinion on clip art and do you intend to use it in your documents?**

7 | Controlling Page Appearance

Lesson Time: 45 minutes

Lesson Objectives:

In this lesson, you will control a document's page setup and its overall appearance.

You will:

- Control page layout.
- Apply a page border and color.
- Add a watermark.
- Add headers and footers.

Introduction

In the previous lessons, you have inserted text, tables, and graphics into your document. Now that the page contents are complete, you can adjust the page appearance to suit your output needs. In this lesson, you will control the appearance of pages in a document.

Altering the appearance of a page to suit the content helps to make an impression. A formal letter needs to have a simple border, whereas a certificate can have a colorful border. By changing a variety of page options, you can get the content to fit on the page, as well as enhance the document's appearance and readability.

TOPIC A

Control Page Layout

In this lesson, you will control page appearance. Adjusting various aspects of the overall page layout is one of the most common ways to adjust the appearance of document pages. In this topic, you will control page layout.

Just as an architect decides on the layout of a new home, keeping in mind visual appeal and convenience, you must define the layout of your documents to ensure that the content appears as you want it to. Word allows you to specify page margins and orientation, helping to ensure that you are pleased with the print output.

Margin Options

The Margins gallery, in the Page Setup group of the Page Layout tab, has a list of predefined margin types. You can apply a predefined margin type by selecting one from the Margins gallery if you want to change all the margins in a document at once. You can also customize the size of each margin individually to increase or decrease the text area, add white space, or adjust the overall page layout.

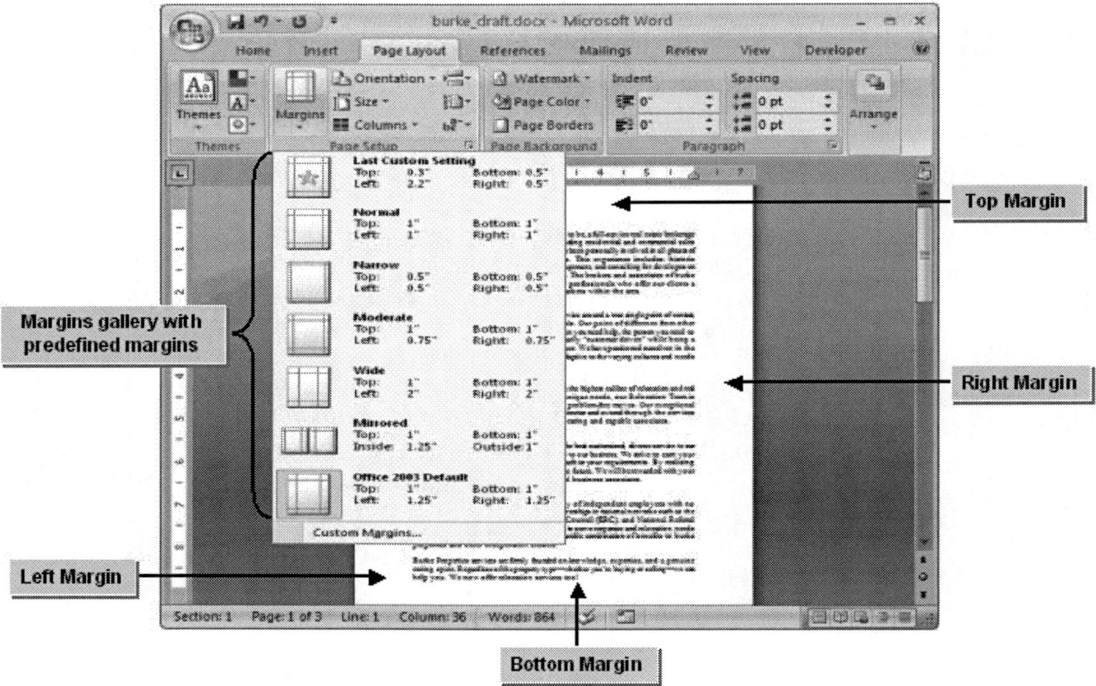

***Figure 7-1:** Preset margins in the Margins gallery.*

Default Margin Types

Word has six default margin types. Each type sets different dimensions for the various margins in a document.

Margin Type	Description
Normal	Top, bottom, inside, and outside margins are at a distance of 1 inch from the page border. (Inside and outside margins refer to the edge of the page that would be inside a binding if the document was compiled in book form. Generally, the inside edge is the right edge for left hand pages and vice versa.)
Narrow	Top, bottom, inside, and outside margins are at a distance of 0.5 inches from the page border.
Moderate	Top and bottom margins are at a distance of 1 inch, and inside and outside margins are at a distance of 0.5 inches from the page border.
Wide	Top and bottom margins are at a distance of 1 inch, and inside and outside margins are at a distance of 2 inches from the page border.
Mirrored	Top and bottom margins are at a distance of 1 inch, inside margins are at a distance of 1.25 inches and outside margins are at a distance of 1 inch from the page border.
Office 2003 Default	Top and bottom margins are at a distance of 1 inch, and inside and outside margins are at a distance of 1.25 inches from the page border.

Page Orientation

Definition:

Page orientation is a page setup option that determines whether the information on a page will be laid out vertically, in Portrait orientation, or horizontally, in Landscape orientation. The orientation setting affects the overall layout of the text on a page and affects how the document will print.

Example:

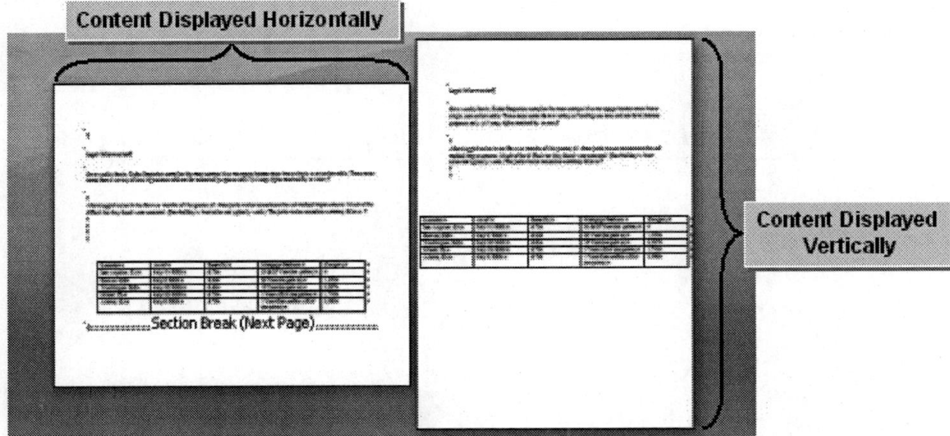

Figure 7-2: Page Orientation can be either vertical or horizontal.

Vertical Alignment Options

You can control how text on a page is aligned vertically between the top and bottom margins. The options are similar to the horizontal alignment options available for paragraph formatting. Vertical alignment options work the same way for both Portrait and Landscape page orientations.

Vertical Alignment Option	*Description*
Top	Positions the text along the top margin of the page. It is the default vertical alignment setting.
Center	Positions the page's text in the center of the page, providing equal amounts of white space above and below the text.
Justified	Adds equal amounts of white space between each paragraph so that text appears to fill the page.
Bottom	Aligns the text along the bottom margin of the page.

Paper Size

The *Paper Size* option modifies the width and height of the document to suit the paper used when printing. In Word, the Size options are found on the Page Layout tab, which is located in the Page Setup group. The Size drop-down list contains various paper sizes to resize your document. You can also specify a custom paper size by selecting the More Paper Sizes option and setting the necessary options in the Page Setup dialog box.

Paper Size Options

The Size drop-down list in the Page Setup group of the Page Layout tab has a number of paper size options. Each option has a predefined width and height specified in inches. The sizes correspond to standard sizes for paper and envelopes that are commonly used in business correspondence in various countries and geographic regions. The following table lists some of the most common paper and envelope sizes.

Paper Size	*Width In Inches*	*Height In Inches*
Letter	8.5	11
Legal	8.5	14
Executive	7.25	10.5
A3	11.69	16.54
A4	8.27	11.69
A5	5.83	8.27
11 x 17	11	17
Envelope #10	4.12	9.5

The Page Setup Dialog Box

The Page Setup dialog box contains options to modify the overall page layout of the document.

Page Setup Tab	Description
Margins	Enables you to set margins and orientation and to determine the content capacity of the page. It also contains options to specify whether the suggested modification is to be applied to the whole document or just to specific pages.
Paper	Allows you to modify the paper size and the paper source for printing. It also enables you to access the Display tab in the Word Options dialog box, which contains options to set the display of the paper for printing.
Layout	Enables you to modify the layout of a particular section and set different styles for the heading regions. It also lets you set a page border.

Page Breaks

A *page break* is used to split the content of a page at a specific location and move the remaining content to the next page automatically. Word inserts automatic, or soft, page breaks at the end of each page to accommodate additional text when there is too much of it to fit on a single page. However, there may be times when you want to force a page break in order to control where a page ends. In those cases, you can insert a manual page break using the Breaks button in the Page Setup group of the Page Layout tab, or by pressing Ctrl+Enter. A manual page break appears as a non-printing dotted line.

Automatic page breaks are primarily determined by margin settings in the Page Setup dialog box. Automatic page breaks display differently in different document views.

How to Control Page Layout

Procedure Reference: Insert or Delete a Manual Page Break

To insert or delete a manual page break:

1. Place the insertion point where you want to insert a manual page break.

2. On the Page Layout tab, in the Page Setup group, click Breaks and select Page, or press Ctrl+Enter.

3. You can delete a manual page break by pressing Backspace or Delete as you would delete any other typed character. It is helpful to show the formatting marks so that the page break is visible.

Procedure Reference: Control Page Layout

To control page layout:

1. Open the document in which the page layout needs to be changed.

2. Change the page orientation.

   - On the Page Layout tab in editing view or the Print Preview tab in Print Preview, in the Page Setup group, click Orientation and select Portrait or Landscape.

   - Or, change the page orientation using the Page Setup dialog box.

     a. On the Page Layout tab, in the Page Setup group, click the Dialog Box Launcher button.

     b. In the Page Setup dialog box, on the Margins tab, in the Orientation section, select Portrait or Landscape to position the page vertically or horizontally, respectively.

     c. Click OK.

3. Set the paper size.

   - On the Page Layout tab in editing view or the Print Preview tab in Print Preview, in the Page Setup group, click Size and select a size.

   - Or, open the Page Setup dialog box, select the Paper tab, and select the paper size from the Paper Size drop-down list. To customize the paper size, enter the custom values in the Width and Height text boxes. Click OK.

4. Set the page margins.

   - On the Page Layout tab in the Editing view or the Print Preview tab in Print Preview, in the Page Setup group, click Margins and select an option.

   - Drag the margin markers on the vertical and horizontal rulers. To set an exact measurement, hold Alt as you drag.

> The left and right margin markers might be obscured by the left and right indent markers, so you might want to temporarily move the indent markers before setting the margins.

   - Or, open the Page Setup dialog box, and on the Margins tab, specify the measurements for the Top, Bottom, Left, and Right margins in the respective spin boxes, and click OK.

5. Set the vertical alignment.

    a. Open the Page Setup dialog box and select the Layout tab.

    b. In the Page section, select the desired alignment from the Vertical Alignment drop-down list and click OK.

White Space Between Pages

After inserting a page break, there is generally extra white space at the bottom of the page before the break. You can hide the white space between pages to reduce the amount of scrolling you need to do to see all the document text when you are in Print Layout view. When you position the mouse pointer between the two pages, the mouse pointer changes into a Hide White Space icon or a Show White Space icon. You can toggle between Hide White Space and Show White Space modes by double-clicking or by pressing Ctrl and clicking.

ACTIVITY 7-1

Inserting Manual Page Breaks

Data Files:

Stockholder Report.docx

Before You Begin:

From the C:\084893Data\Controlling Page Appearance folder, open Stockholder Report.docx.

Scenario:

The annual report's editor says that you can use four pages of the report for your overview text. The document contains multiple pages. The only problem is that the pages are breaking in places that you don't want them to and separating data that really needs to stay together. After you adjust the page breaks, you would like to be able to scroll quickly through the document to check the overall text flow from page to page, to see if there are any pages that you should combine.

What You Do	How You Do It
1. Insert a manual page break before the heading "REVIEW".	a. Use the Status Bar to verify that there are currently four pages in the document. Page: 1 of 4 b. Scroll down to the bottom of page 1. c. At the bottom of page 1, **place the insertion point before the heading "REVIEW OF YEAR RESULTS"**. d. On the Page Layout tab, in the Page Setup group, click Breaks and **select Page.**
2. Insert a manual page break before the heading "ADVANTAGE".	a. Scroll down to the end of page 2. b. On page 2, **place the insertion point before the heading "ADVANTAGE"**. c. **Press Ctrl+Enter** to insert a manual page break.

d. **Verify that there are now five pages in the document.**

Page: 3 of 5

3. **Hide the white space between page 2 and page 3.**

   a. **Position the insertion point over the automatic page break between pages 2 and 3** to display the Hide White Space icon.

   b. **Double-click** to hide the extra white space between the two pages.

   c. **Scroll up and down** to verify that you can see continuous text.

4. **Delete the extra page break** so that the text "ADVANTAGE" can fit on the preceding page.

   a. At the end of page 2, **place the insertion point before the Page Break formatting mark.**

   b. **Press Delete** to delete the page break.

5. **Redisplay the white space between page 2 and page 3.**

   a. **Scroll down** to display the end of page 2.

   b. **Position the mouse pointer over the automatic page break between pages 2 and 3** to display the Show White Space icon.

   c. **Double-click** to redisplay the white space.

   d. **Save the file as *My Stockholder Report.docx* and close the document.**

ACTIVITY 7-2

Changing a Document's Layout

Data Files:

Certificate.docx

Before You Begin:

From the C:\084893Data\Controlling Page Appearance folder, open Certificate.docx.

Conditions:

You have a printer installed.

Scenario:

Your manager has put you in charge of creating a new sales certificate. She has provided you with the text and requested that you print the certificate horizontally on 11" x 17" paper. Also, she wants you to include at least 1.5 inches of blank space at the top and bottom of the certificate. You want to neatly align the content in the certificate.

What You Do	**How You Do It**

1. **Set the document's orientation to Landscape.**

   a. On the Page Layout tab, in the Page Setup group, **click Orientation and select Landscape.**

   b. On the View tab, in the Zoom group, **click Zoom.**

   c. In the Zoom dialog box, in the Zoom To section, **select Whole Page and click OK.**

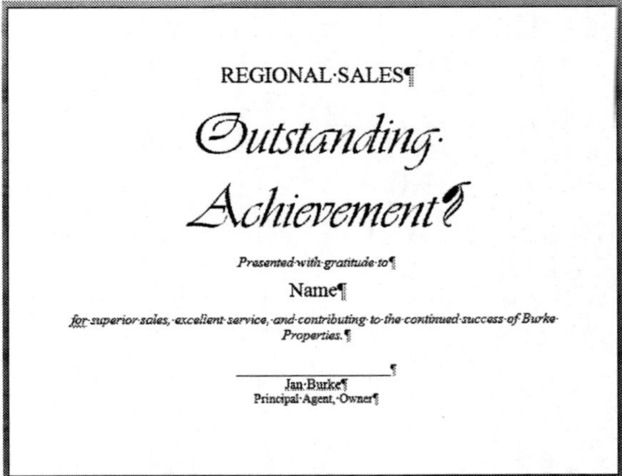

<table>
<tr>
<td>

2. **Change the size of the paper to 11″ x 17″.**

</td>
<td>

a. On the Page Layout tab, in the Page Setup group, **click the Dialog Box Launcher button.**

b. In the Page Setup dialog box, **select the Paper tab.**

c. **From the Paper Size drop-down list, select 11x17.**

d. **Verify that the Height and Width values are 11 and 17 and click OK.**

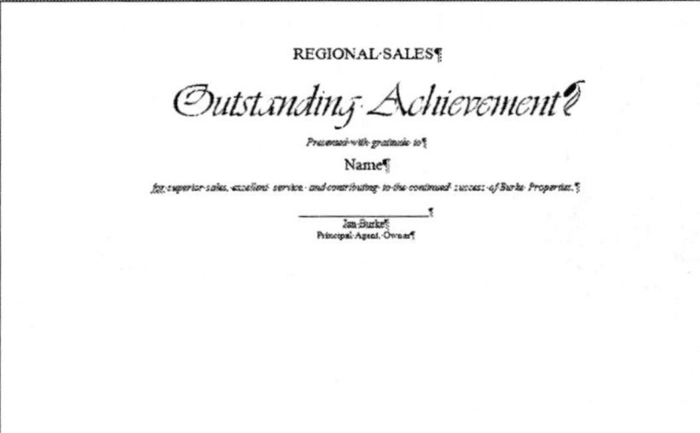

</td>
</tr>
<tr>
<td>

3. **Set the top and bottom margins of the document to 1.5 inches.**

</td>
<td>

a. In the Page Setup group, **click the Dialog Box Launcher button.**

b. **Select the Margins tab.**

c. **Triple-click in the Top text box, type *1.5* and press Tab.**

d. In the Bottom text box, **type *1.5* and press Tab.**

e. **Click OK.**

</td>
</tr>
<tr>
<td>

4. **Center the text vertically on the page.**

</td>
<td>

a. In the Page Setup group, **click the Dialog Box Launcher button.**

b. In the Page Setup dialog box, **select the Layout tab.**

</td>
</tr>
</table>

c. In the Page section, from the Vertical Alignment drop-down list, **select Center and click OK.**

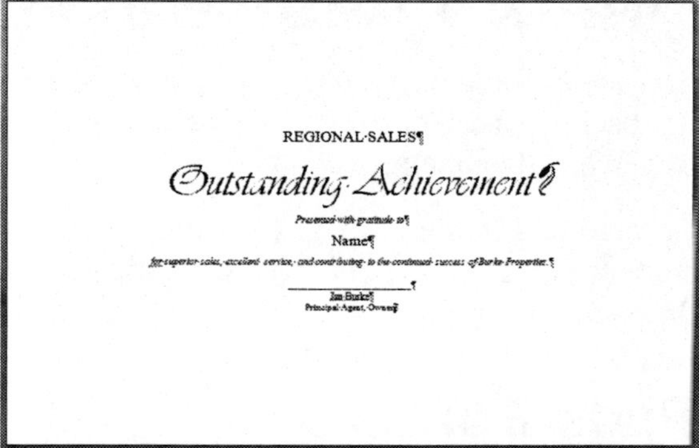

d. **Save the file as *My Certificate.docx***

TOPIC B

Apply a Page Border and Color

You have changed the page orientation, paper size, and margins. Now, you want to enhance the background elements in the document. In this topic, you will apply a page border and color to a Word document.

Colored and bordered pages not only add visual interest to a document, but they also make the content stand out clearly. This can help readers locate critical ideas quickly and stay focused as they read it.

Page Borders

Definition:

Page Borders are formatting tools that apply an outline to a document. Page Borders can be any style, color, or width. Borders can be applied either to the whole document or to a specific section. Page borders can only be applied in the margin area of a document. You can apply page borders to a document using the options in the Borders And Shading dialog box. You can add or remove borders on all four sides of a document.

Example:

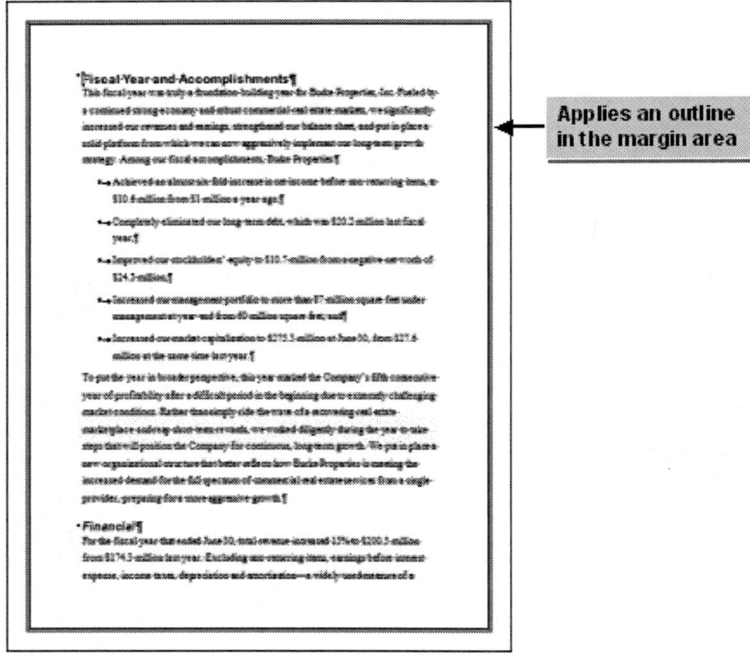

Figure 7-3: A border applied to the entire page.

Border Types

Word provides users with two types of borders: Line borders and Art borders.

Border Type	Description
Line Borders	Word applies a Line page border as a default border style. When you select a line page border, it is applied as a box or as a custom style. The style, color, and width of the line can be modified.
Art Borders	Word contains numerous seasonal and professional Art page borders that can serve as printed frames for certificates, awards, or diplomas. When you select an Art page border, it's applied as a box or custom style. The size and color of the art in the border can also be modified.

Page Color

Page Color is a formatting tool that applies a shade to the background of the entire page. You can apply any shade to the page by choosing the desired color from the Page Color gallery. In Word, you can access the Page Color option by clicking Page Color in the Page Background group of the Page Layout tab.

How to Apply a Page Border and Color

Procedure Reference: Apply a Page Border

To apply a border to a page:

1. Select the page in which the border needs to be displayed.
2. Display the Page Border tab of the Borders And Shading dialog box.
   - On the Home tab, in the Paragraph group, from the Borders drop-down list, select Borders And Shading and select the Page Border tab.
   - Or, on the Page Layout tab, in the Page Background group, click Page Borders.
3. Set border options.
   - Select the desired Setting, Style, Color, and Width options for a line page border.
   - From the Art drop-down list, select an art border and set the color and width options.
4. If necessary, in the Preview area, click the border buttons to add or remove borders. This sets the new style as a custom border that is applied to all of the borders in the document.
5. Click OK to apply the border.

Procedure Reference: Apply a Page Color

To apply a page color:

1. On the Page Layout tab, in the Page Background group, click Page Color.
2. From the Page Color gallery, select the desired shade.
3. If necessary, from the Page Color gallery, select More Colors and select a different color.

ACTIVITY 7-3

Applying an Art Page Border

Before You Begin:

My Certificate.docx is open.

Scenario:

The content of the sales certificate has been approved by your manager. You now have to make the certificate visually appealing so it looks impressive when presented to the employees. Since your company has installed a new color printer, you have the option of using colors to enhance the visual appeal.

What You Do	**How You Do It**
1. **Apply an Art page border to the top and bottom of the page.**	a. On the Page Layout tab, in the Page Background group, **click Page Borders.**
	b. In the Borders And Shading dialog box, in the Art drop-down list, **scroll down and select the Music Notes border.**
	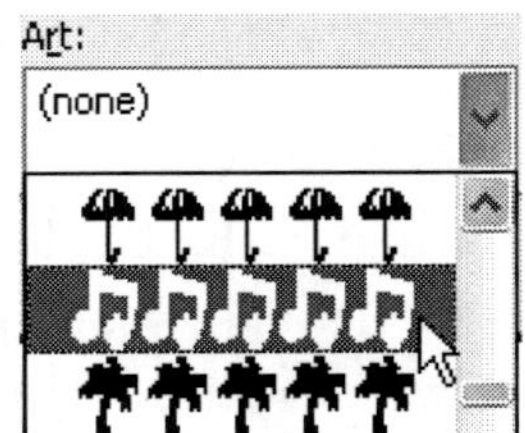
	c. From the Color drop-down list, in the Standard Colors section, **select the first shade** to make the border dark red.
	d. **Click OK** to apply the Art border and to close the dialog box.
2. **Apply background color to the certificate.**	a. On the Page Layout tab, in the Page Background group, **click Page Color.**

b. In the Page Color gallery, in the Theme Colors section, in the third row in the last column, **select Orange, Accent 6, Lighter 60%.**

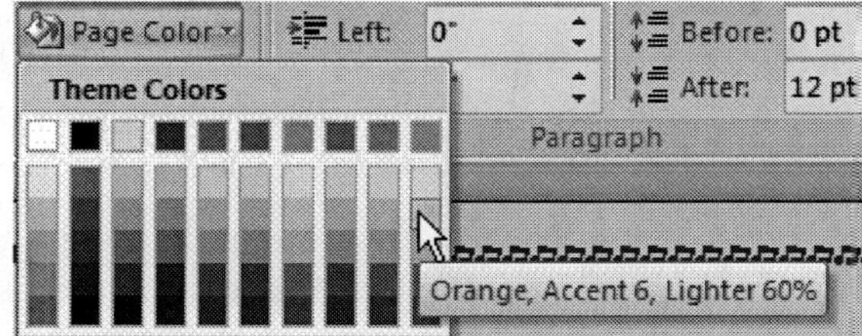

c. **Save the document and close it.**

TOPIC C

Add Watermarks

In the previous topic you applied page background options such as page color and a page border. Another way to modify the page background is to add a watermark. In this topic, you will add a watermark.

Sometimes you need to ensure that warning or informational messages appear throughout a document, and, in particular, that the messages appear with the text itself, not only in the margins as with a header or footer. For example, you might need to protect your copyright to a particular document by ensuring that the word "copyright" appears on any photocopy made from the document. Or, there might be a legal requirement that you differentiate draft or internal material from material that is publicly available. A watermark is a common publication convention that enables you to meet these requirements, protect your information, and produce professional-looking document output in a simple and effective way.

Watermarks

Definition:

A *watermark* is a translucent image of either text or a graphic that appears behind the primary text in a document when the document is printed or previewed. In Word, if you add a watermark to a document, it is applied to all its pages. Click Watermark on the Page Layout tab, in the Page Background group to add, delete, or customize an existing watermark.

Example:

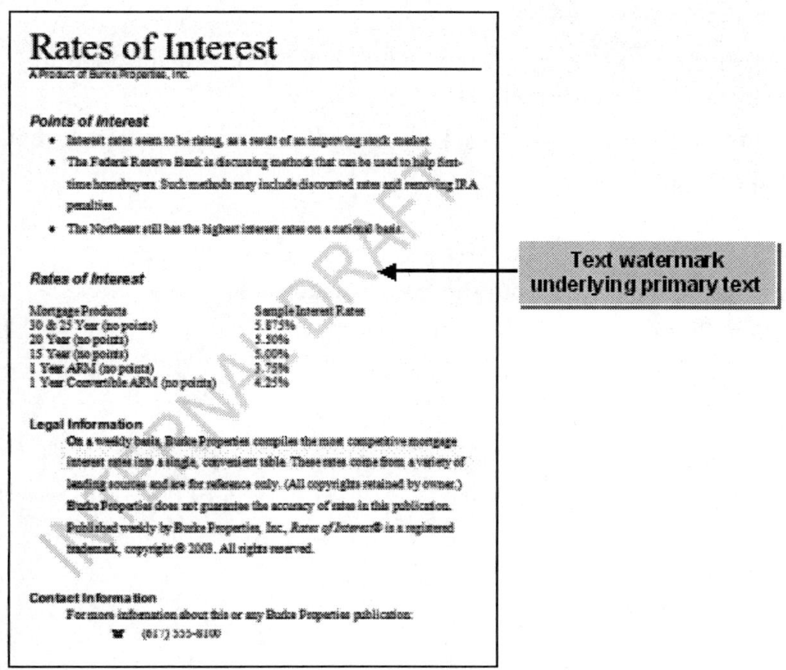

Figure 7-4: Text as a watermark.

The Printed Watermark Dialog Box

The Printed Watermark dialog box contains options you can use to customize the watermarks that are displayed in a document. You can select a picture to use as a picture watermark, and you can scale the picture and adjust its translucency. You can specify the text and font appearance for a text watermark, and you can decide if text watermarks run diagonally or horizontally.

How to Add a Watermark

Procedure Reference: Add a Text Watermark

To add a text watermark:

1. On the Page Layout tab, in the Page Background group, click Watermark.
2. In the Watermark gallery, select one of the default watermarks, or click Custom Watermark.
3. If you clicked Custom Watermark, in the Printed Watermark dialog box, select the Text Watermark option and, if desired, customize the watermark.
4. Click OK to insert the text watermark.

Procedure Reference: Add a Picture Watermark

To add a picture watermark:

1. On the Page Layout tab, in the Page Background group, click Watermark.
2. In the Watermark gallery, click Custom Watermark.
3. In the Printed Watermark dialog box, select the Picture Watermark option and then click Select Picture.

4. In the Insert Picture dialog box, select a picture and click Insert.

5. If necessary, customize the picture watermark.

    ●   In the Scale text box, enter a value to which the picture should be scaled, or from the drop-down list, select a predefined value.

    ●   Check or uncheck the Washout check box to set the picture as opaque or translucent.

6. Click OK to insert the picture watermark.

Removing a Watermark

To remove a watermark, in the Page Layout tab, from the Page Background group, click Watermark and click Remove Watermark.

ACTIVITY 7-4

Adding a Text Watermark

Data Files:

Rates of Interest.docx

Before You Begin:

From the C:\084893Data\Controlling Page Appearance folder, open Rates of Interest.docx.

Scenario:

The Rates of Interest document is ready to be reviewed. However, the last time you sent something for review, it was printed without your approval and several thousand copies had to be thrown away. To ensure that doesn't happen again, you should mark the document as an INTERNAL DRAFT so that there is no question about the document's current status.

What You Do	How You Do It
1. **Display the Printed Watermark dialog box.**	a. On the Page Layout tab, in the Page Background group, **click Watermark.**
	b. In the Watermark gallery, **select Custom Watermark.**
2. **Apply the text "INTERNAL DRAFT" as a watermark.**	a. In the Printed Watermark dialog box, **select Text Watermark.**
	b. In the Text text box, **select ASAP,** which is displayed by default.
	c. **Type *INTERNAL DRAFT***
	d. **Click the Font drop-down arrow.**
	e. **Press A** to display the fonts that start with A.

f. **Select Arial** to change the font to Arial.

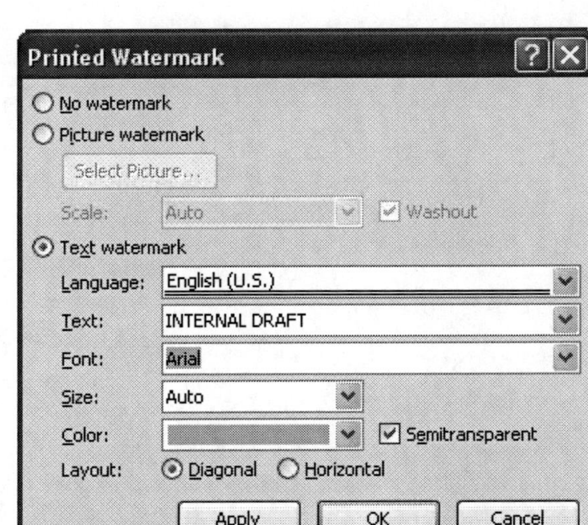

g. **Click OK** to add the text watermark to the document's background.

h. **Scroll down** to view the result.

i. **Save the document as** *My Rates of Interest.docx* **and close it.**

TOPIC D
Add Headers and Footers

You have added background information to your document. Another way to add consistent information throughout the document is to add headers and footers. In this topic, you will add headers and footers.

You just got back from a trade show and have a stack of papers to review. One article in particular is very interesting, but nowhere in the document is there any indication of who wrote it or how many pages it has. Adding page numbers and other useful information to the header and footer area helps to orient the reader to the information contained in the document.

Headers and Footers

A *header* is the area in a page's top margin and a *footer* is the area in a page's bottom margin. Headers and footers can contain textual or graphical information that is common to all or to some of the pages in a document. Common header and footer information includes titles, dates, and page numbers. This information can be entered into one of the three sections of headers and footers, namely, the Left, Center, and Right sections. The Header & Footer group within the Insert tab is used to insert the desired header and footer information into a document.

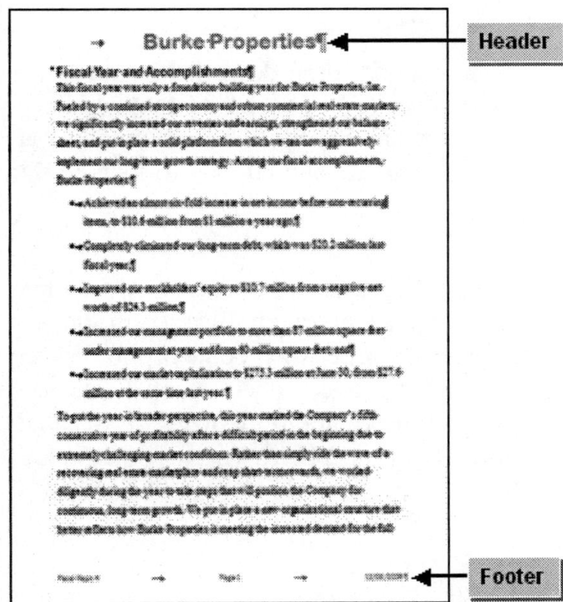

Figure 7-5: A document with a header and a footer inserted.

Header & Footer Tools Design Contextual Tab

The Header & Footer Tools Design contextual tab contains numerous option groups to work with in the header and footer.

Group	*Description*
Header & Footer	Contains built-in header, footer, and page number styles that can be used to format the header and footer.
Insert	Contains options which enable you to insert objects like pictures and clip art. You can also insert the date and time using options in this group.
Navigation	Contains options to navigate to the header, footer, and the previous or next sections in a document.
Options	Contains options to apply different formatting to the header or footer on the first page, odd and even pages, or to the entire document.
Position	Contains options to modify the size of the header and footer. This group also allows you to align the content of the header or footer.
Close	Enables you to close the header or footer section and return to normal document editing.

Page Number Options

In Word, you can insert page numbers by using the Page Number drop-down list in the Header & Footer group of the Insert tab or from the Header & Footer Tools Design contextual tab. The Page Numbers drop-down list provides options to insert and modify the page numbers at the top or bottom of pages, or in the left or right margins. You can add custom formats to the page numbers or remove page numbers entirely.

Fields

A field is a placeholder for data that is used to dynamically represent information. A field may include the current date, time, or page number. Though fields are normally inserted in the header and footer sections of the document, they can be inserted between content, too. When the insertion point is within a field, the field's background turns gray to help identify it as a field. Usually, a field is automatically updated based on the information provided. To manually update a field, you can press F9. Also, using the Field dialog box enables you to insert fields quickly.

Page Number Format Options

Using the Header & Footer group of the Header & Footer Tools Design contextual tab, you can change the page number formats from the default "1, 2, 3" format to any of the following Arabic or Roman numeral formats:

- -1-, -2-, -3-,...
- a, b, c,...
- A, B, C,...
- i, ii, iii,...
- I, II, III,...

How to Add Headers and Footers

Procedure Reference: Add Headers and Footers

To add headers and footers to a document:

1. Display the header and footer section.

    - Double-click either the top or bottom of the document within the text area to display the header or the footer section.

    - Or, on the Insert tab, in the Header & Footer group, click Header or Footer and select Edit Header or Edit Footer.

2. Insert the header or footer text.

    - In the appropriate Header or Footer section, type the text.

    - If necessary, align your text to the center or the right of the header or footer section.

        - Place the insertion pointer in the header section and press Tab.

        - Or, use the Alignment Tab dialog box.

    - Or, insert a built-in header or footer style.

        a. On the Header & Footer Tools Design contextual tab, in the Header & Footer group, click Header and select a built-in header or footer style.

        b. Select the default text and type the header or footer text.

Procedure Reference: Change Page Number Formats

To change page number formats:

1. Display the header or footer containing the page number.

2. On the Header & Footer Tools Design contextual tab, in the Header & Footer group, click Page Number and select Format Page Numbers.

3. In the Page Number Format dialog box, from the Number Format drop-down list, select the desired format.

4. Click OK to set the new format and to close the dialog box.

Procedure Reference: Add a Date and Time to the Header or Footer

To add a date and time to the header or footer:

1. Select the header or footer in which the date and time needs to be included.

2. On the Header & Footer Tools Design contextual tab, in the Insert group, click Date & Time.

3. In the Date And Time dialog box, in the Available Formats list box, select the desired date and time format.

4. If necessary, check the Update Automatically check box, to update the date and time automatically according to the computer's system settings.

5. Click OK to insert the date and time.

6. To modify the date and time format, select the date and time item in the header or footer, click Date & Time, and select a different format.

Procedure Reference: Modify Headers or Footers

To modify a header or footer:

1. Double-click the header or footer you want to modify.

2. On the Header & Footer Tools Design contextual tab, set the necessary formats.

   - In the Header & Footer group, select a built-in format for the header or footer.
   - In the Insert group, insert the date and time, a picture, or clip art.
   - In the Navigation group, select an option to navigate to the desired header or footer in the current document section or another document section.
   - In the Options group, specify the format for headers and footers on specific pages.
     - Check the Different First Page check box to apply a different header and footer to the first page of the document.
     - Check the Different Odd & Even Pages check box to apply a different set of formats to the header and footer in the odd and even pages.
     - Check or uncheck the Show Document Text check box to display or hide the text in the document.
   - In the Position group, set the header and footer dimensions.
     - In the Header From Top spin box, specify the desired values using the up and down arrows.
     - In the Footer From Bottom spin box, specify the desired values using the up and down arrows.
     - Click Insert Alignment Tab, and in the Alignment Tab dialog box, set the alignment and leaders.

3. In the Close group, click Close Header And Footer.

ACTIVITY 7-5

Adding Headers and Footers

Data Files:

Annual Overview.docx

Before You Begin:

From the C:\084893Data\Controlling Page Appearance folder, open Annual Overview.docx.

Scenario:

Your manager is giving a presentation at the Relo Expo conference and would like to leave the company's annual overview behind as a handout so potential clients can peruse last year's successes. Your job is to make the handout more identifiable as a Burke Properties document. You find it would be helpful if the page numbers and current date and time are displayed in the handout. Additionally, you wish to draw special attention to the first page.

What You Do	How You Do It
1. **Insert the text "Burke Properties Overview" at the center of the header.**	a. **Double-click the top of the document** to display the header and footer sections.
	b. **Press Tab** to move the insertion point to the center of the header section.
	c. **Type *BURKE PROPERTIES OVERVIEW***
2. **Add a footer that includes the current date and time, the conference name, and the page number.**	a. On the Header & Footer Tools Design contextual tab, in the Navigation group, **click Go To Footer.**
	b. In the Header & Footer group, **click Page Number and select Bottom Of Page.**
	c. In the Bottom Of Page gallery, **scroll down, and click Accent Bar 4.**
	d. In the footer section, **type *Relo Expo* and press Tab** to separate the page number from the text.
	e. In the Insert group, **click Date & Time.**

f. In the Date And Time dialog box, in the Available Formats list box, **select the twelfth format that includes both the date and the time.**

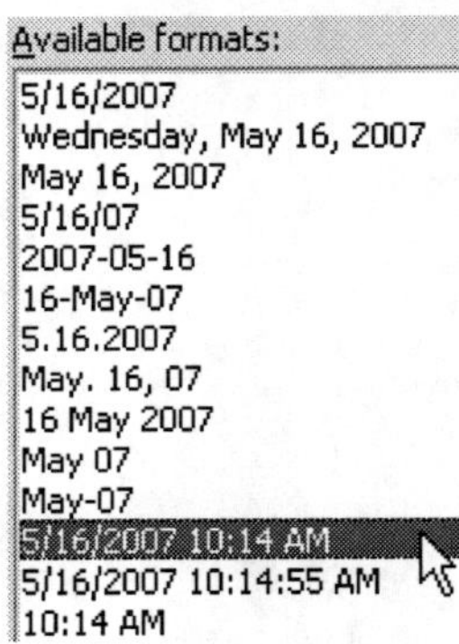

g. **Click OK** to insert the selected date and time.

h. **Press Tab** to center the date and time.

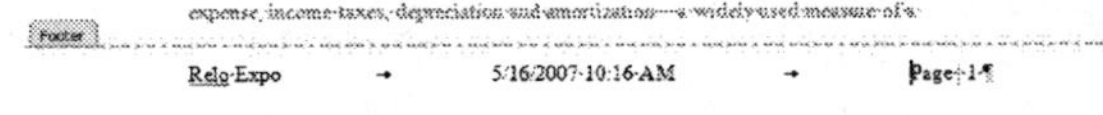

---

3. **Add a different header and footer to the first page.**

a. In the Options group, **check the Different First Page check box.**

b. **In the Navigation group, click Go To Header.**

c. In the Header & Footer group, **click Header and select Alphabet.**

d. In the Header section, **triple-click before the existing heading** to select it **and type *BURKE PROPERTIES ANNUAL OVERVIEW***

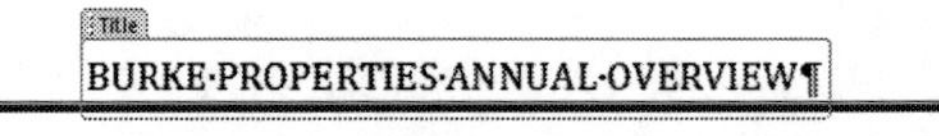

e. In the Header & Footer group, **click Footer and select Alphabet.**

f. **Click before the text "[Type text]" and type *RELO EXPO***

g. In the Close group, **click Close Header And Footer.**

---

4. **Preview the content of the new header and footer.**

a. **Click the Office button and choose Print→Print Preview.**

b. **Observe that the separate headers and footers are seen.**

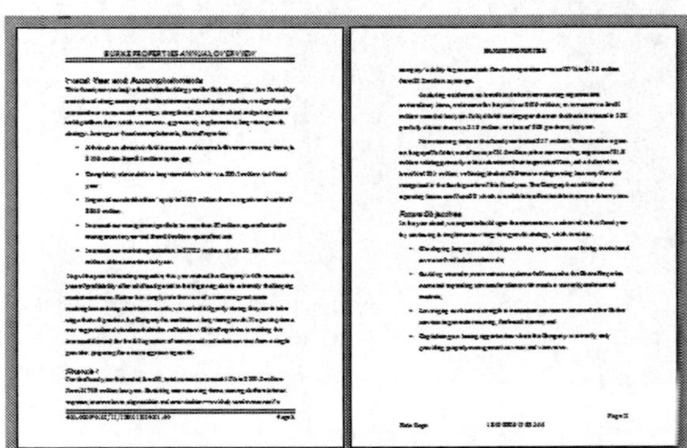

c. **Close Print Preview.**

d. **Save the file as *My Annual Overview.docx***

ACTIVITY 7-6
Modifying Headers and Footers

Before You Begin:
Annual Overview.docx is open.

Scenario:
As you read through your document, you find that only the first page of the document briefs you about the overview, and the remaining pages include general information on Burke Properties. Also, you decide to change the page number format.

What You Do	How You Do It
1. In the body of the document, **change the header to read "Burke Properties Annual Report".**	a. At the top of the second page, **double-click the header section** to edit the text in the header area.
	b. **Select the word "Overview" and press Delete.**
	c. **Type *ANNUAL REPORT***
2. **Edit the footer to display only the page number at the center.**	a. On the Header & Footer Tools Design contextual tab, in the Navigation group, **click Go To Footer.**
	b. **Select all the text in the footer section and press Delete.**
	c. **Press Tab** to place the insertion point in the center.
	d. In the Header & Footer group, **click Page Number and select Bottom Of Page.**
	e. In the Bottom Of Page gallery, **scroll down** and, from the Plain Number section, **select Brackets 1.**
	f. In the Header & Footer group, **click Page Number and select Format Page Numbers.**

g. In the Page Number Format dialog box, from the Number Format drop-down list, **select the second option.**

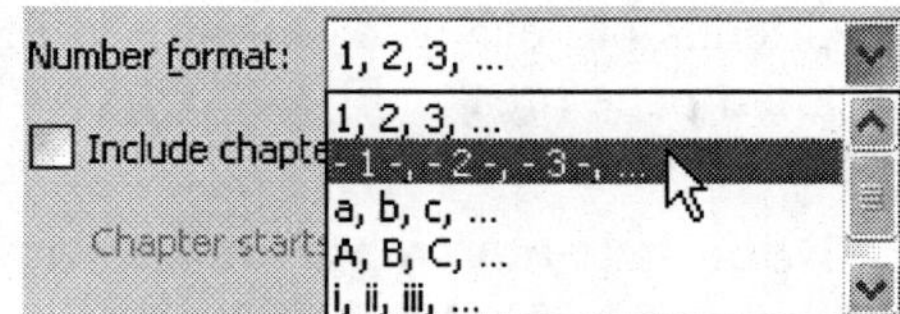

h. **Click OK** to apply the changes.

i. In the Close group, **click Close Header And Footer.**

j. **Preview, save, and close the file.**

Lesson 7 Follow-up

In this lesson, you used a variety of page setup methods to arrange content on the page. You set the page orientation, changed margin settings, added headers and footers, applied page borders, and inserted page breaks. These skills will help you to present the document with suitable finishing touches.

1. **How will you take advantage of the various page layout options to enhance printed documents such as letters, reports, handouts, minutes, or itineraries?**

2. **Considering your job needs, do you anticipate modifying a document's page setup options when you first create the document or waiting until you are almost finished with it? Why?**

8 | Proofing a Document

Lesson Time: 45 minutes

Lesson Objectives:

In this lesson, you will proof documents to make them more accurate.

You will:

- Check spelling, grammar, and word count in a document.
- Enhance textual meaning using the Thesaurus.
- Customize AutoCorrect options.

Introduction

You have entered and formatted text, tables, and graphics in a document, and adjusted the overall document appearance. The final step before your document is complete is to proofread the document and make corrections and updates as needed. In this lesson, you will use proofing tools that help you correct common typing mistakes and enhance your word choices.

There is no substitute for thoroughly proofreading your own work and applying your own creative judgement to finalize its contents. However, Microsoft Word's built-in proofing tools can simplify some of the mechanics of proofreading, and can also help you revise your document electronically without having to reach for a dictionary or other reference book. By using these proofing tools effectively, you can ensure your document's accuracy while you streamline the overall process of proofreading and finalizing a document.

TOPIC A

Check Spelling, Grammar, and Word Count

In this lesson, you will proofread documents to make them more accurate and more interesting. Probably the single most common proofreading task is to check the spelling in a document, followed closely by checking grammar and overall document length. In this topic, you will check the spelling, grammar, and word count.

One of the many benefits of electronic word processing is that it makes it easy to correct the minor spelling and other typographical errors that every typist makes. Plus, it can save you valuable time because you can thoroughly review the overall document rather than spending your time identifying and correcting spelling and usage manually as you go. No matter how you choose to use them, Word's spelling, grammar, and text count tools can make your documents more accurate, and speed the process of identifying and eliminating typographical mistakes.

Spelling And Grammar Check Options

Microsoft Word provides electronic tools that enable you to check the spelling and grammar usage in your document against a built-in word list and set of grammar rules. To check your work, you can click the Spelling & Grammar button in the Proofing group on the Review tab. You can also click the Spelling And Grammar Check button on the Microsoft Office Status Bar and choose the desired option from the shortcut menu. Another option is to right-click the underlined word and choose the desired option from the shortcut menu.

Options in the Spelling And Grammar Dialog Box

The Spelling And Grammar dialog box offers various options to help you edit grammar and spelling.

Option	*Function*
Not In Dictionary	Displays the words or sentences that have been identified as errors by Word.
Suggestions	Displays a list of possible correct options.
Check Grammar	Enables you to check for erroneous grammar along with a spell check.
Ignore Once	Enables you to skip the occurrence of the error this time but find the next occurrence. In this way, you can correct found text on a case-by-case basis.
Ignore All/Ignore Rule	Enables you to leave all instances of the highlighted text unchanged and continue searching for the next error.
Add To Dictionary	Enables you to add the occurrence to the dictionary. This will allow Word to recognize the occurrence as correct any time you spell check in the future.
Change	Replaces the found text with the selected correction in the Suggestions list box.

Option	Function
Change All	Replaces all occurrences of the highlighted text with the suggested word at the same time. While using the Change All option, users need to be careful as you can easily make changes you didn't intend to make.
AutoCorrect	Replaces all instances of erroneous words or sentences automatically.
Options	Displays the Proofing tab in the Word Options dialog box. This tab contains options to check and proof the document for errors.
Undo	Enables you to undo the previous edit if you want to revert to the original text.

The Main Dictionary

Word uses the *Main Dictionary* to check a document's spelling. As you type, or when you run the Spelling And Grammar tool, Word compares your spelling to the list of terms stored in the main dictionary. If you have misspelled a word, or if you have used a specialized word that is not in the dictionary, the spell checker will give you a list of possible suggestions.

Custom Dictionaries

You can also create custom dictionaries that include words specific to a particular subject matter. You can add entries to Word's default custom dictionary, Custom.dic, or you can create or import other custom dictionaries. To manage custom dictionaries, open the Word Options dialog box, select the Proofing tab, and click Custom Dictionaries. For more information on custom dictionaries, see the Microsoft Office Word Help system.

The Readability Statistics Dialog Box

Readability statistics are ratings that provide a measurement of the complexity level of text. If you have enabled readability statistics in Word, the Readability Statistics dialog box is displayed after you check the grammar. This dialog box provides detailed information on the total and average number of words, sentences, and paragraphs in your document, and reports the readability scores for the content in your document.

Grading of Readability Scores

There are different readability analysis methods. The readability scores in Word are based on the Flesch Reading Ease and the Flesch-Kincaid Grade Level scales. These scales help to evaluate the readability and complexity of the document based on the average number of syllables per word and words per sentence. Flesch Reading Ease scores text as a single number, with higher scores indicating easier reading. The Flesch-Kincaid Grade Level categorizes the text according to United States public school grade-level reading standards. The two scales use slightly different formulas and have a reverse correlation; a low reading ease score correlates to a high grade level and vice versa. The readability scores should match the target reading audience; some government agencies require that public documents match a target readability range.

In addition, Word's readability statistics also tell you how many sentences use passive voice ("the ball was thrown by the boy") instead of active voice ("the boy threw the ball"). Most writing experts recommend using active voice in the majority of sentences.

The Word Count Dialog Box

Microsoft Word can help you ensure that a document you write fits within content length limits by providing you with a running word count. When you click Words on the Microsoft Office Status Bar, or the Word Count button in the proofing group, the Word Count dialog box opens. The Word Count dialog box keeps track of the number of pages, words, characters, paragraphs, and lines in the document. As you enter text in a document, Word also displays a live word count on the Microsoft Office Status Bar.

How to Check Spelling, Grammar, and Word Count

Procedure Reference: Enable Readability Statistics

To enable Readability Statistics:

1. Click the Office button and click Word Options.
2. In the Word Options dialog box, select the Proofing category.
3. In the When Correcting Spelling And Grammar In Word section, check the Show Readability Statistics check box.
4. Click OK.

Procedure Reference: Check Spelling and Grammar

To check spelling and grammar:

1. To check spelling and grammar as you type.
   - Using the contextual menu,
     a. Right-click text with a red wavy underline (for spelling errors) or a green wavy underline (for grammar errors).
     b. Select the desired correction from the context menu.
   - Click the contextual Spelling And Grammar Check button that appears in the Microsoft Office Status Bar when Word detects a spelling or grammar error.
2. Otherwise, to check the entire document, position the insertion point at the beginning of the document; to check a selection, select the text.
3. Display the Spelling And Grammar dialog box.
   - On the Review tab, in the Proofing group, click Spelling & Grammar.
   - Press F7.
   - Or, right-click text with a wavy underline and choose Spelling or Grammar.
4. Click a button to proceed with the first spelling or grammar error displayed.
5. Make the appropriate selection depending on whether it is a spelling correction or a grammar correction.
6. Sometimes the appropriate correction does not appear. If you need to edit text directly in the document, click in the document, edit the text, and then click Resume in the dialog box.
7. Edit the other errors in the document as per your discretion.
8. Click OK to close the dialog box when you are done.
9. If the Readability Statistics dialog box appears, review the statistics and click OK.

Procedure Reference: Check Word Count

To check the number of words in a Word document:

1. If you want to count the number of words in a specific section of text, select it; otherwise, simply place your insertion point anywhere in the document.

2. Display the Word Count dialog box.

    - On the Review tab, in the Proofing group, click the Word Count button.

    - On the Microsoft Office Status Bar, click the Words button.

    - Or, press Ctrl+Shift+G.

3. When you have finished reviewing the word count, click Close.

ACTIVITY 8-1

Checking a Document's Spelling, Grammar, and Length

Data Files:

Relocation Letter.docx

Before You Begin

From the C:\084893Data\Proofing a Document folder, open Relocation Letter.docx.

Scenario:

You typed your text quickly because you know that you can return and correct any mistakes after you enter all of the document's content. Now, you need to check for and correct any typographical errors. You also need to ensure that the document is not overly difficult to read, and that the overall length of the document will fit in the 300–word limit available to you in the client mailing.

What You Do	How You Do It
1. **Enable the Readability Statistics option.**	a. **Click the Office button and then click Word Options.**
	b. In the Word Options dialog box, **select the Proofing category.**
	c. **Scroll down** and in the When Correcting Spelling And Grammar In Word section, **check the Show Readability Statistics check box.**

When correcting spelling and grammar in Word

☑ Check spelling as you type
☑ Use contextual spelling
☑ Mark grammar errors as you type
☑ Check grammar with spelling
☑ Show readability statistics
Writing Style: Grammar Only ▾ [Settings...]

	d. **Click OK** to close the Word Options dialog box.

2. **Correct the misspelled word and the grammar error using the shortcut menu.**

   a. **Verify that the insertion point is placed at the beginning of the document.**

   b. On the Microsoft Office Status Bar, **click the Spelling And Grammar Check button.**

   c. From the shortcut menu, **choose Inquiring** to replace the misspelled word.

   d. The Readability Statistics dialog box appears. **Click OK** to close it.

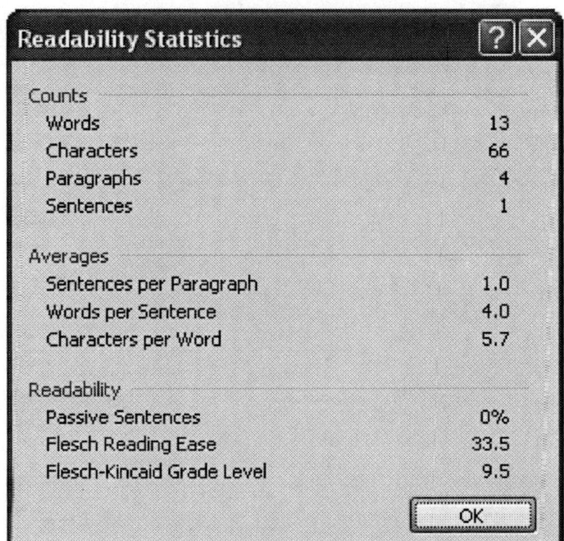

   e. In the second sentence, **right-click anywhere in the text "objective of Burke Properties are" and choose objective of Burke Properties is** to correct the grammar error.

3. **Make changes to the document using the Spelling And Grammar tool.**

   a. **Position the insertion point at the beginning of the document.**

   b. On the Review tab, in the Proofing group, **click Spelling & Grammar.**

   c. **Click Change** to replace "complament" with "complement".

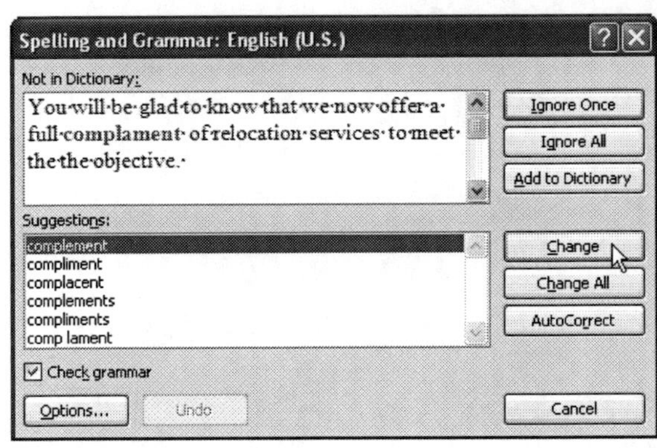

   d. The next error is a repeated word "the". **Click Delete** to delete the repeated word.

   e. Next, the word "TeamServe" is not recognized, but it is correct. **Click Ignore All** to skip all occurrences of this word.

   f. The word "Beantown" is correct. **Click Ignore All** to skip all occurrences of this word.

   g. The word "BurkeBuddy" is correct. **Click Ignore All.**

   h. Because it should be capitalized, "the" appears in green. **Click Change** to replace "the" with "The".

   i. The next error indicates a subject-verb agreement grammar problem. **Click Change** to replace "is" with "are".

   j. **Review the Readability Statistics and click OK** to close the Readability Statistics dialog box.

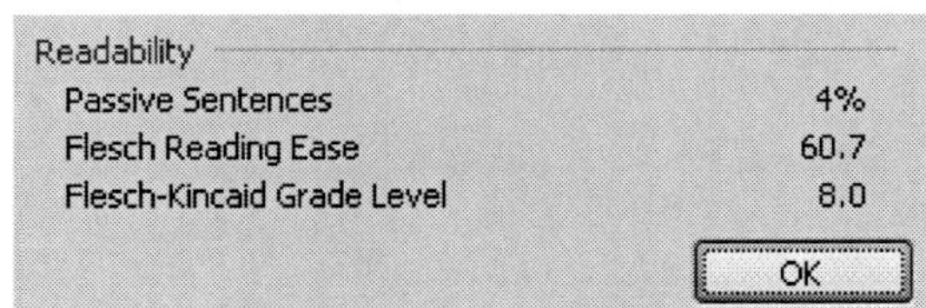

4. Check the number of words in the document.

   a. In the Proofing group, **click the Word Count button.** 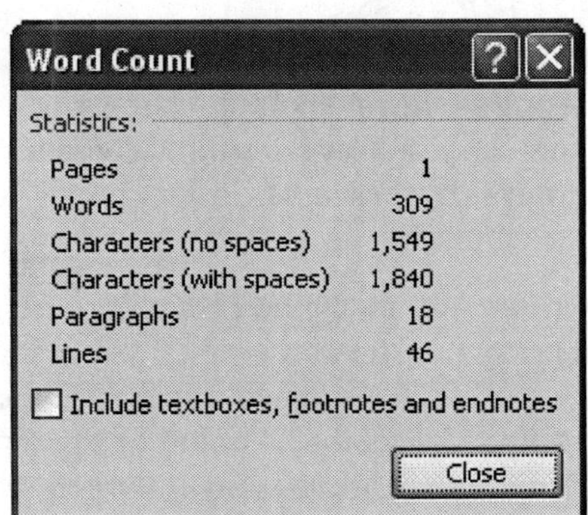

   b. There are 309 words in the document, which is over the limit. **click Close.**

5. Count the words in the last paragraph.

   a. **Triple-click the paragraph that begins "It is our objective"** to select it.

   b. On the Microsoft Office Status Bar, **verify that the live word count is 30.**

6. Delete the last paragraph to reduce the word count.

   a. **Delete the last paragraph.**

   b. In the Proofing group, **click the Word Count button.**

   c. Observe that you are beneath the word count limit and **click Close.**

   d. **Save the document as *My Relocation Letter.docx***

TOPIC B

Enhance Textual Meaning Using the Thesaurus

Microsoft Word's built-in spelling checker is an electronic substitute for a physical dictionary. Similarly, you can use Word's online Thesaurus as a substitute for another common writer's reference, a physical thesaurus. In this topic, you will use Word's built-in Thesaurus to help find the right words.

You have written a draft memo promoting the useful features of your company's new email program. When you re-read the draft, you find that you described nearly every feature the same way — "useful". A greater variety of words could make the memo more readable, but it is difficult to think of a large number of appropriate synonyms on your own. A thesaurus is a specialized reference work that many writers use to help them find alternate word choices, and with Word's electronic Thesaurus, this helpful writer's resource is just a couple of clicks away.

The Thesaurus

Definition:

A *thesaurus* is a reference tool that gives you a collection of synonyms and antonyms. Unlike a dictionary, a thesaurus does not provide the definition of a word. Word includes an electronic Thesaurus that you can use to make alternate choices for the word usage in your document. Access the Thesaurus from the Proofing group of the Review tab. The Thesaurus is available in various languages such as English (U.S.), French (France), and Spanish (International Sort).

Example:

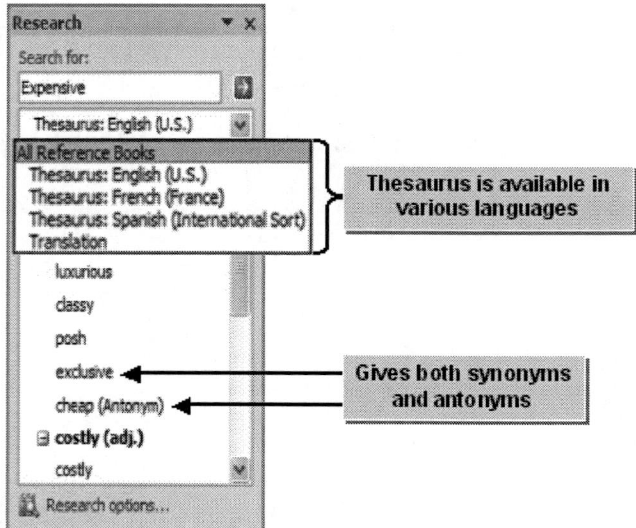

***Figure 8-1:** Word's Thesaurus is available in different languages.*

The Research Task Pane

The *Research task pane* lets you look up information using a wide variety of online references including various dictionaries and thesauruses. You can even use it to translate text from one language to another. Because the Research task pane provides access to a number of web-based research books and reference sites, you will need an active Internet connection to use all of its research options. Open the Research task pane by clicking the Research button on the Review tab.

The Research Options Dialog Box

The Research Options link located at the bottom of the Research task pane opens the Research Options dialog box so that you can customize the reference books and research sites you want to access.

Options	Description
Services	Lists the various reference books and other services you can use to search for information. Checking the desired Reference Book check box displays options in the All Reference Books list.
Add Services	Opens the Add Services dialog box that allows you to specify the website address from where you wish to avail services for research options. The desired service can also be chosen from the Advertised Services list box. However, the list of Advertised Services are provided by Microsoft's Discovery Server. Once the desired service is added, it is displayed in the Services list box.
Update/Remove	Displays the Update Or Remove Services dialog box that enables the user to update the reference books or to remove unnecessary reference books from the Services list box.
Parental Control	Enables you to control the change of options in the Research task pane. Protecting the research options by setting a password on the Parental Control prevents unauthorized users from making changes to the research services.
Properties	Displays the Service Properties dialog box that contains information about the name of the reference book, its description, copyright details, and the name of its provider. The Properties button is active only after a particular reference book has been selected from the Services list box.

How to Use the Thesaurus

Procedure Reference: Select Synonyms or Antonyms from the Thesaurus

To select synonyms or antonyms from the Thesaurus:

1. Select the desired word. Be sure the word is spelled correctly; Word will only suggest synonyms for words in its dictionary.

2. Display the Thesaurus in the Research task pane.

   - Right-click the word for which you want to find a synonym or antonym and choose Synonyms→Thesaurus.

   - On the Review tab, in the Proofing group, click Thesaurus.

   - Hold down Alt and double-click the desired word.

   - Or, press Shift+F7.

3. In the Research task pane, in the Thesaurus: English (U.S.) list box, point to the desired synonym or antonym, click the drop-down arrow, and choose Insert to replace the existing word.

If you accidentally click the word, just click the Previous Search or Back button to return to the previous list of options.

4. To choose from a list of the most common synonyms while you are typing, right-click the word, choose Synonyms, and select the synonym.

Procedure Reference: Change Research Options

To change research options:

1. On the Review tab, in the Proofing group, click Research.

2. In the Research task pane, click Research Options.

3. In the Research Options dialog box, change the research options.

   - In the Services list box, check or uncheck the desired check box to display or hide the corresponding service option in the Research task pane.

   - Add the desired service to the available services.

     a. In the Research Options dialog box, click Add Services.

     b. In the Add Services dialog box, in the Address box, type the URL of an Office 2007 compatible service, or select an advertised service from the Advertised Services list.

     c. Click Add and follow the on-screen instructions.

   - If necessary, insert a password to restrict use of the Research task pane.

     a. In the Research Options dialog box, click Parental Control.

     b. In the Parental Control dialog box, check the Turn On Content Filtering To Make Services Block Offensive Results check box to activate the Specify A Password For The Parental Control Settings section.

     c. In the Specify A Password For The Parental Control Settings text box, enter the desired password.

     d. Click OK.

ACTIVITY 8-2

Using the Thesaurus to Replace a Word

Before You Begin

My Relocation Letter.docx is open.

Scenario:

You are writing a letter to your client. You find that some words have been used frequently. You wish to avoid this rut and replace the words with similar ones. Additionally, you have decided to add a research service to Word's Research Options dialog box in order to complete necessary research quickly when writing client letters.

What You Do	**How You Do It**
1. Replace the word "objective" in the second paragraph with its synonym "goal".	a. In the second paragraph, **right-click the word "objective".**
	b. **Choose Synonyms→Goal.**
2. Replace the word "fair" in the last paragraph with the word "impartial".	a. **Scroll down to the end of the page.**
	b. In the last paragraph, **right-click "fair" and choose Synonyms→Thesaurus.**
	c. In the Research task pane, in the Thesaurus: English (U.S) list box, **scroll up and place the mouse pointer over "impartial", click the drop-down arrow, and select Insert.**

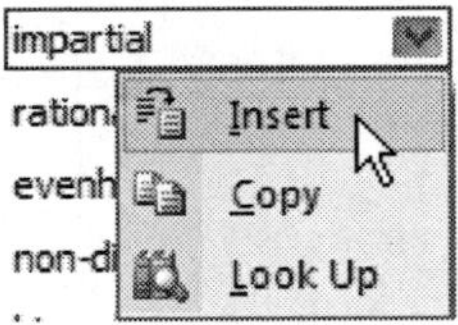

<table>
<tr><td valign="top">3.</td><td>Add a service to Word's Research Options.</td><td valign="top">a.</td><td>In the Research task pane, click the Research Options link.</td></tr>
<tr><td></td><td></td><td valign="top">b.</td><td>In the Research Options dialog box, click Add Services.</td></tr>
<tr><td></td><td></td><td valign="top">c.</td><td>In the Add Services dialog box, in the Address text box, type http:// integrate.factiva.com/research/ query.asmx</td></tr>
<tr><td></td><td></td><td valign="top">d.</td><td>Click Add.</td></tr>
<tr><td></td><td></td><td valign="top">e.</td><td>In the Factiva, by Dow Jones Setup dialog box, click Continue and then click Install.</td></tr>
<tr><td></td><td></td><td valign="top">f.</td><td>In the Add Services message box, click OK.</td></tr>
<tr><td></td><td></td><td valign="top">g.</td><td>In the Research Options dialog box, scroll down and verify that Factiva iWorks™ appears in the list under Research Sites.</td></tr>
<tr><td></td><td></td><td valign="top">h.</td><td>Click OK to close the Research Options dialog box.</td></tr>
<tr><td></td><td></td><td valign="top">i.</td><td>Clear the Research task pane, and save and close the file.</td></tr>
</table>

TOPIC C

Customize AutoCorrect Options

In the first topics in this lesson, you used built-in reference sources to revise and correct your work. Word's AutoCorrect options also help you correct your work and you can customize the options so that the AutoCorrect feature better meets your needs. In this topic, you will customize AutoCorrect options.

The AutoCorrect feature is extremely helpful for catching and fixing minor typos without requiring you to perform a complete spellcheck. However, the default behavior of AutoCorrect might not meet your needs. A common example could be specialized words or abbreviations that you use frequently in your work environment, such as a product or company name with unique capitalization, that you do not want automatically corrected. The many configurable options in the AutoCorrect dialog box enable you to set up AutoCorrect to your exact specifications and make your data entry even more accurate and efficient.

The AutoCorrect Dialog Box

The *AutoCorrect dialog box* contains a series of tabs that you can use to control AutoCorrect behavior.

Tab	Provides Options To
AutoCorrect	Automatically edit typographical or capitalization errors.
Math AutoCorrect	Automatically replace expressions with the corresponding symbols.
AutoFormat As You Type	Automatically format the document text as you type.
AutoFormat	Automatically format the style of the document.
Smart Tags	Automatically locate certain data types using hidden smart tags.

The AutoCorrect Tab

The *AutoCorrect tab* in the AutoCorrect options dialog box has a number of options that enable you to automatically edit the typographical or capitalization errors in a document.

Option	Enables You To
Show AutoCorrect Options Buttons	Displays the AutoCorrect Options button whenever the AutoCorrect feature edits a typographical error.
Correct Two Initial Capitals	Corrects errors of entering two initial capitals for a word.
Capitalize First Letter Of Sentences	Automatically capitalize the initial letter of every sentence.
Capitalize First Letter Of Table Cells	Automatically capitalizes the initial letter of words entered in each cell of a table.
Capitalize Names Of Days	Automatically capitalizes the initial letter of days.

Option	Enables You To
Correct Accidental Usage Of Caps Lock Key	Automatically corrects the casing of letters in a sentence if Caps Lock is accidentally activated.
Exceptions	Makes a list of word or characters that you would like to retain as you type them.
Replace Text As You Type	Replaces common typographical errors or other key combinations with designated words or characters. For example, as a shortcut for words you type frequently, such as your company's name, you can enter an abbreviation that Word will expand to the full word or phrase. You should not add words that already exist in the list as shortcuts for other words. However, you can add words and special characters to this list, but you cannot add shapes or other graphic objects.

How to Customize AutoCorrect Options

Procedure Reference: Customize AutoCorrect Options

To customize AutoCorrect options:

1. Display the AutoCorrect dialog box.

    a. Click the Office button and click Word Options.

    b. In the Word Options dialog box, select the Proofing category.

    c. In the AutoCorrect Options section, click the AutoCorrect Options button.

2. In the AutoCorrect dialog box, check or uncheck the desired options.

3. To add exceptions to AutoCorrect rules, click Exceptions, type your exceptions on the appropriate tab, and click OK.

4. To add shortcut text to replace as you type, enter the shortcut text in the Replace section, enter the full text in the With section, and click Add.

5. Click OK to close the AutoCorrect dialog box.

6. Click OK to close the Word Options dialog box.

ACTIVITY 8-3

Customizing the AutoCorrect Options

Data Files:

Relocation Staff.docx

Before You Begin

From the C:\084893Data\Proofing A Document folder, open Relocation Staff.docx.

Scenario:

You are creating a document that gives information about Burke Properties. As you will have multiple occurrences of the word Burke Properties and Facility Request Form, using an abbreviation that automatically changes to the desired word would be helpful. Also, you need to insert more text into the document.

What You Do	How You Do It
1. **Display the AutoCorrect dialog box.**	a. **Click the Office button and then click Word Options.**
	b. In the Word Options dialog box, **select the Proofing category.**
	c. In the AutoCorrect Options section, **click AutoCorrect Options.**
2. **Set up data-entry shortcuts for Burke Properties and Facility Request Form.**	a. In the AutoCorrect dialog box, in the Replace Text As You Type section, in the Replace text box, **type *bp* and press Tab** to move to the With text box.
	b. In the With text box, **type *Burke Properties* and click Add.**

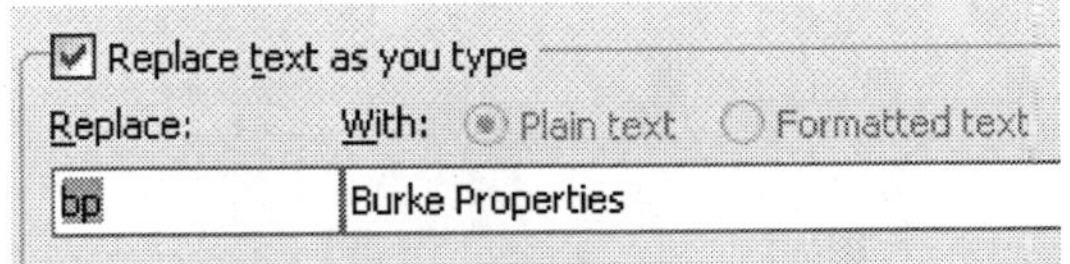

	c. In the Replace text box, **type *frf* and press Tab** to move to the With text box.

d. In the With text box, **type *Facility Request Form* and click Add.**

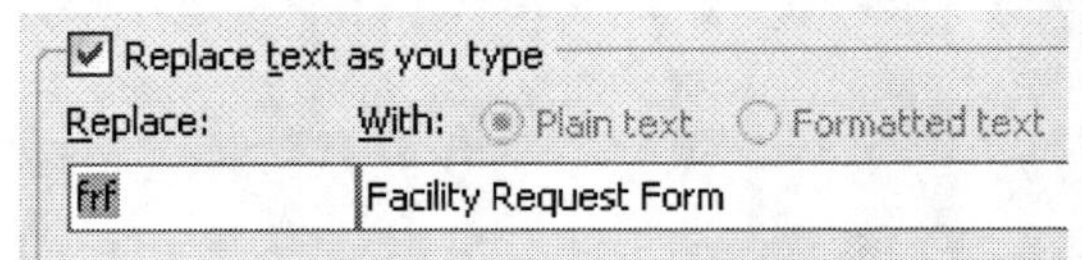

e. **Click OK** to close the AutoCorrect dialog box.

f. **Click OK** to close the Word Options dialog box.

---

3. **Include the necessary text in the document.**

a. In the third paragraph of the document, under the subtitle, "Facility Request Form", **type *We have created a frf* and press Spacebar.**

b. Observe that frf was replaced with Facility Request Form.

c. **Type *for you to use whenever you require assistance.***

d. **Position the insertion point below the heading "Contact Information:".**

e. **Type *For information regarding bp* and press Spacebar.**

f. Observe that bp has been changed to Burke Properties.

g. **Type *publications, contact:***

h. **Save the document as *My Relocation Staff.docx* and close the document.**

Lesson 8 Follow-up

In this lesson, you used several proofing tools, including the spellchecker, Thesaurus, and AutoCorrect to make your documents more accurate. These tools assist you with the mechanics of data entry and data revision so that you can concentrate on the creative aspects of your writing and produce clear, accurate, and interesting documents with a minimum amount of effort.

1. **Which proofing tools do you think will help you create more accurate documents?**

2. **How do you think the proofing tools will impact the way you proof documents?**

Follow-up

In this course you created, edited, and enhanced standard documents using Microsoft® Word 2007.

1. **Which feature in Word will help the most as you create documents?**

2. **What automatic features in Word will you use most often?**

3. **How will you use Word's Help options?**

What's Next?

After completing this course, students may be interested in expanding their knowledge of Microsoft® Word 2007 by taking Element K's *Microsoft® Office Word 2007: Level 2 (Second Edition)* and *Microsoft® Office Word 2007: Level 3 (Second Edition)* courses.

Lesson Labs

Due to classroom setup constraints, some labs cannot be keyed in sequence immediately following their associated lesson. Your instructor will tell you whether your labs can be practiced immediately following the lesson or whether they require separate setup from the main lesson content.

Lesson 1 Lab 1

Creating a New Word Document

Activity Time: 15 minutes

Scenario:

You work in the Human Resources department and your manager has handed you her hand-written notes regarding a new HMO that will soon be available. She has asked you to type it as an interoffice memo that, when printed, can be distributed to all employees.

Your manager's notes read as follows: We will soon offer a new HMO plan from Doctors Unlimited to all employees. Costs are lower without sacrificing coverage. More details to come.

---

1. **Open a new blank document and set the view to Print Layout mode.**

---

2. In the new document, **type the memo text.**

---

3. In the C:\084893Data\Creating a Basic Document folder, **save the document as *My Memo.docx* in the default format.**

---

4. **Preview the document.**

---

5. **Print a copy of the document.**

---

6. **Close the document.**

Lesson 2 Lab 1

Editing a Document

Activity Time: 10 minutes

Data Files:

Facility Request.docx, Building Security.docx

Before You Begin:
Word is running with no documents open.

Scenario:
You have been given the responsibility to edit procedure documents for the Human Resources department. The draft document is available.

1. **Open C:\084893Data\Editing a Document\Facility Request.docx.**

2. In the first sentence, **"We have created a Facility Request Form", after Facility Request Form, insert the text *(FRF)***

3. Throughout the document, **replace any remaining instances of "Facility Request Form" with "FRF".**

4. **Delete the paragraph that begins with "More than any other document."**

5. **Open Building Security.docx from the same location.**

6. **Copy the contact names and phone numbers from the end of Building Security.docx and paste them at the bottom of Facility Request.docx.**

7. **Save the document as *My Facility Request.docx* and then close both documents.**

Lesson 3 Lab 1

Formatting Text

Activity Time: 10 minutes

Data Files:

Formatting Text.docx

Setup:

From the C:\084893Data\Formatting Text folder, open Formatting Text.docx.

Scenario:

As the Assistant Manager of Books & Beyond, one of your responsibilities is to apply the finishing touch to all your official correspondence. You've now been given a typed document to which you need to apply text formatting.

1. Format the title "Books & Beyond" as Tahoma, 18 pt., Bold.

2. Change the format of "Welcome to Our World of Reading and Relaxation" to Tahoma, 14 pt., Italic.

3. Change the font of the underlined heading "Books" to Tahoma, 11 pt.

4. Copy the formatting of the heading "Books" and apply it to the headings "Music" and "Other Media".

5. Highlight the text of your choice and then change the highlight color to a color of your choice.

6. Save the file as *My Formatting Text.docx* and close it.

Lesson 4 Lab 1

Formatting Paragraphs

Activity Time: 10 minutes

Data Files:

Formatting Paragraphs.docx

Setup:

From the C:\084893Data\Formatting Paragraphs folder, open Formatting Paragraphs.docx.

Scenario:

Since your last assignment went so well, your manager at Books & Beyond is anxious to get you started on your next task. She now needs you to enhance the document's readability and visual appeal.

1. **Apply the Heading 1 style to the heading "What is Books & Beyond" and center it.**

2. **Apply the Heading 2 style to "Other Special Services", and "How Are We Doing So Far?"**

3. **Change the paragraph spacing so that there is a 6-point space after each paragraph heading.**

4. Under "Other Special Services", **format the paragraphs as a bulleted list.**

5. For the "Top Music Categories" tabbed text, **change the left indent to 1.75 inches, the right indent to 4.5 inches, and center the heading.**

6. In the tabbed text, **set the right tab stops at 3.25 inches and 4.25 inches.**

7. **Apply a box border to the "Top Music Categories" tabbed text.**

8. **Replace all instances of underline text formatting with double-underlined bold italics.**

9. **Save the document as *My Formatting Paragraphs.docx* and close it.**

Lesson 5 Lab 1

Adding Tables

Activity Time: 10 minutes

Data Files:

Table.docx, enus_084893_05_solution.zip

Setup:

From the C:\084893Data\Adding Tables folder, open Table.docx.

Scenario:

Your next task is to create a formatted table using a document provided by your coworker. You have also been asked to add a new table that includes the various types of top-selling audio books.

1. **Convert the Top Selling Music Categories tabbed text into a table.**

2. **Format it using a table style and other formatting options of your choice.**

3. Below the Top Selling Audio Book Categories heading, **create a new table to accommodate the following text:**

Category	*Sales*
Biography	1,589
Fiction	3,972
Hobby/Recreation	2,975
Youth	756

4. **Apply a format to the new table so that its formatting matches the other table.**

5. **Save the document as *My Table.docx* and then close it.**

Lesson 6 Lab 1

Inserting Graphic Elements

Activity Time: 10 minutes

Data Files:

Graphic Elements.docx

Setup:

From the C:\084893Data\Inserting Graphic Elements folder, open Graphic Elements.docx.

Scenario:

You need to complete a one-page flyer promoting the upcoming "Get Published" seminar. You decide to include the appropriate image clip for the flyer and corresponding copyright and trademark symbols. You also decide to mark the document as a free issue so that there is no question about its status.

1. **Open the Graphic Elements document.**

2. **Insert a book-related clip art image at the top of the document and resize it to keep the flyer to one page.**

3. In the first paragraph of text, **insert the corresponding symbols after the words "copyright" and "trademark".**

4. **Save the document as *My Graphic Elements.docx* and then close it.**

Lesson 7 Lab 1

Controlling Page Appearance

Activity Time: 10 minutes

Data Files:

Page Setup.docx, enus_084893_07_solution.zip

Before You Begin:

Open the Page Setup.docx file, from the C:\084893Data\Controlling Page Appearance folder.

Scenario:

The shop manager made some formatting suggestions for the "Get Published" flyer. You need to implement those suggestions. As you preview the document, you also wish to change its orientation.

1. **Reduce the margins to get the text on a single page.**

2. **Add a box border to the page.**

3. In the footer area, **insert the date.**

4. **Change the document's orientation to Landscape.**

5. **Preview the document to verify your results.**

6. **Save the document as** *My Page Setup.docx* **and then close it.**

Lesson 8 Lab 1

Proofing a Document

Activity Time: 10 minutes

Data Files:

Proofing.docx

Setup:

Open the Proofing.docx file, from the C:\084893Data\Proofing a Document folder.

Scenario:

You have completed a client letter and it's time to proof the document. There are some typing mistakes, so make corrections, as necessary. Also, you wish to add the word BurkeBuddy to the burke properties.dic dictionary. You also need to check the word count so that it is under 200 words.

1. Spell check the document, correcting spelling and grammar errors as needed.

2. Use the Thesaurus to change some instances of the word "business" with synonyms of your choice.

3. Verify that the letter has 200 words or fewer.

4. Save the letter as *My Proofing.docx* and then close it.

Solutions

Glossary

AutoCorrect
A feature that is used to fix common typographical errors, apply common formatting to characters, and identify data types, thereby enhancing the value of your text.

border
A decorative line or pattern that is displayed around objects.

bulleted list
A list that is used to denote a group of equally significant items.

clip art
An illustration with a simple two-dimensional effect.

Clipboard group
A group on the Home tab containing options to cut, paste, and copy text and its styles in a document.

Clipboard task pane
Lists the objects that have been copied or cut from the document.

Compatibility Checker
A feature that enables you to identify the compatibility of objects used in your .docx document when it is saved in an earlier version of Word.

contextual tabs
Tabs with specialized commands that are displayed when the object they operate on, such as a table, picture, or shape, is selected.

Dialog Box Launchers
Small arrow buttons occupying the bottom-right corner of certain groups on the Ribbon that launch dialog boxes with commands specific to the features found in that group.

font
A predefined typeface that can be used for formatting characters. Each font has a unique design and character spacing.

footer
The blank area in a page's bottom margin. Ordinarily repeated throughout a document, a footer can contain textual or graphical information to provide context for the reader.

Format Painter
A formatting tool that allows you to duplicate the character or paragraph formatting in the selected text to a new text selection.

formatting mark
Document indicators that are non-printable and are displayed in the text area.

Galleries
Libraries that list the varying outcomes of using certain commands found within the Ribbon.

header

The blank area in a page's top margin. Ordinarily repeated throughout a document, a header can contain textual or graphical information to provide context for the reader.

Home tab

A tab that contains the most commonly used commands that enable you to start working with a Word document.

illustrations

Graphic elements that provide visual representation of the text.

indent

An alignment technique to align the left and right edges of a paragraph without changing the margins for the entire document.

Insert tab

A tab that enables quick access to different object types such as charts, tables, and pictures that can be added to a document.

line break

A formatting mark used to end the current line before it wraps to the next line automatically without starting a new paragraph.

list

A data grouping method in which the items in the group are displayed one after the other.

Live Preview

A feature that enables users to preview the results of applying design and formatting changes to a document in real time, without actually applying it.

Main Dictionary

The primary dictionary used to check a document's spelling. The Main Dictionary is neither editable nor viewable.

margin

The blank area surrounding the text along the top, bottom, left, and right edges of a page.

Microsoft Office Status Bar

A bar that displays a number of options relating to document functionality in a well-organized manner.

Mini toolbar

A toolbar that contains commonly used commands for formatting text.

numbered list

A list that is used to denote a ranking or sequence that must be followed to achieve a desired outcome.

Office button

A button that displays a set of options that can be used to work on a document as a whole.

Page Borders

A formatting tool that applies an outline to a document.

page break

Used to split the content of a page at a specific location and move the remaining content to the next page automatically.

Page Color

A formatting tool that applies a shade to the background of a page.

Page Layout tab

A tab that contains commands to customize the pages in a document.

Page Orientation option

A page setup option used to display the elements on the page.

Paper Size

An option to modify the width and height of the document to suit the paper used when printing.

paragraph alignment

An alignment technique that determines how a paragraph is positioned horizontally between the left and right margins.

picture

Graphic representation of a subject.

Print Preview

A view mode that allows you to view the document as it would appear on paper when printed.

Quick Access toolbar

A toolbar that provides easy access to core commands such as save a document, undo a previous action, and repeat a previous action.

Quick Styles

A package of styles that work well together that you can apply to a document as a group.

Quick Tables

A predefined table formatting tool with sample data entered into the cells.

Readability Statistics dialog box

Provides detailed information about a document, including counts, averages, and readability scores of words, characters, paragraphs, and sentences.

Research task pane

Allows you to look up information using a wide variety of online references.

Review tab

A tab that provides various options to review and edit the contents in a document.

Ribbon

A panel on the top portion of a Word document and it contains a selection of easy-to-browse commands that you may need in order to work on a document.

ruler

Measuring tool that is used to align documents.

ScreenTips

A descriptive label that is displayed when you position the mouse pointer over various items, such as a toolbar button, in the program window.

shading

A percentage of color that can be added to the background of objects.

sizing handles

Small circles and squares that appear around the border of a selected clip art image.

smart tags

Hidden tags that are represented by a button that is displayed in response to a given action.

special characters

Punctuation, spacing, and typographical characters. Most special characters are not readily available on the standard keyboard.

style

A named collection if appearance settings that can be applied to sections of a document as a group.

symbols

Character marks that can be used to represent an idea or word such as copyright, trademark, or registered.

tab

A document formatting option that aligns text to a specific horizontal location.

Table Style

A formatting option that contains sets of table-specific formatting options packaged together to apply design and formatting changes to a table all at once.

table

A grid-style container used to organize text, data, or pictures.

table

A grid-style container used to organize text, data, or pictures.

task pane

A small window within the Word environment that provides a list of feature-specific options and commands.

thesaurus

A reference tool that gives you a collection of synonyms and antonyms.

View tab

Provides various options that enable you to switch between different document views.

watermark

A translucent image that appears under the primary text that currently exists.

Word document

A document that is created using the Microsoft Office Word software.

Word Help

A feature that provides you with a quick and easy way to find answers to Word-related queries.

Word Options dialog box

A dialog box that contains a series of tabs, each of which contains commands required to customize the Word environment.

word wrap

A data-entry feature that automatically wraps a long line of text around to the beginning of the next line.

Index

Looking for media files?

They are now conveniently located at www.elementk.com/courseware-file-downloads

Downloading is quick and easy:

1. Visit www.elementk.com/courseware-file-downloads
2. In the search field, type in either the part number or the title
3. Of the courseware titles displayed, choose your title by clicking on the name
4. Links to the data files are located in the middle of the screen
5. Follow the instructions on the screen based upon your web browser

Note that there may be other files available for download in addition to the course files.

Approximate download times:

The amount of time it takes to download your data files will vary according to the file's size and your Internet connection speed. A broadband connection is highly recommended. The average time to download a 10 mb file on a broadband connection is less than 1 minute.